JAGDPANTHER VS SU-100

Eastern Front 1945

DAVID R. HIGGINS

First published in Great Britain in 2014 by Osprey Publishing,
PO Box 883, Oxford, OX1 9PL, UK
PO Box 3985, New York, NY 10185-3985, USA

E-mail: info@ospreypublishing.com

Osprey Publishing is part of the Osprey Group

Print ISBN: 978 1 78200 295 6
PDF ebook ISBN: 978 1 78200 296 3
ePub ebook ISBN: 978 1 78200 587 2

Index by Alan Thatcher
Typeset in ITC Conduit and Adobe Garamond
Maps by bounford.com
Originated by PDQ Media, Bungay, UK
Printed in China through Asia Pacific Offset Ltd

14 15 16 17 18   10 9 8 7 6 5 4 3 2 1

Osprey Publishing is supporting the Woodland Trust, the UK's leading woodland conservation charity, by funding the dedication of trees.

www.ospreypublishing.com

Author's acknowledgements

I would like to thank the following individuals for their kind support, without which this book and my other military history endeavours might not have been possible: Joseph Miranda, editor-in-chief, *Strategy & Tactics* magazine; Colonel (ret.) Jerry D. Morelock, PhD, editor-in-chief, *Armchair General* magazine; Christian Ankerstjerne; Roland Farkas; Magdi Gulyas; Vitaly Kuzmin; the Davis Memorial Library; Valentin Zhukov; Laszlo Pinke; Seth Gaines; Daniel Olsson (Fronthistoriska Föreningen); Nik Cornish at www.stavka.org.uk; and my editor, Nick Reynolds. Any errors or omissions in this work were certainly unintended, and for which I alone bear responsibility.

Author's note

In this book, varying numbering and designation systems are applied to the military units and formations fielded by the various combatants. German-language designations have been retained for German ranks, units and formations, but Soviet and other combatants' ranks, units and formations have been translated into English. Some examples are: 3rd Ukrainian Front; Forty-Sixth Army (spelled out); and I Guards Mechanized Tank Corps (roman numerals).

Glossary

APCBC/HE-T: Armour-Piercing Capped Ballistic Cap/High Explosive – Tracer
APHE-T: Armour-Piercing High Explosive – Tracer
HE: High Explosive
HEAT: High Explosive Anti-Tank
HVAP: High Velocity Armour-Piercing

Editor's note

In this book, metric units of measurement are employed as both the Germans and Soviets used metric during World War II. Following German practice, German weapons designations of 20mm and greater are shown in centimetres. For ease of comparison please refer to the following conversion table:

1m = 1.09yd / 3.28ft
1km = 0.62 miles
1cm = 0.39in
1mm = 0.04in
1kg = 2.20lb / 35.27oz
1 tonne = 0.98 long (UK) tons / 1.10 short (US) tons
1 litre = 0.22 UK gallons / 0.26 US gallons
1kW = 1.34hp (international)

Comparative commissioned ranks

British Army	Heer	Waffen-SS	Soviet
n/a	n/a	*Reichsführer-SS*	Marshal of the Soviet Union
n/a	n/a	n/a	n/a
field marshal	*Generalfeldmarschall*	n/a	n/a
general	*Generaloberst*	*SS-Oberstgruppenführer*	General of the Army
lieutenant-general	*General der Infanterie, etc.*	*SS-Obergruppenführer*	colonel-general
major-general	*Generalleutnant*	*SS-Gruppenführer*	lieutenant-general
brigadier	*Generalmajor*	*SS-Brigadeführer*	major-general
n/a	n/a	*SS-Oberführer*	n/a
colonel	*Oberst*	*SS-Standartenführer*	colonel
lieutenant-colonel	*Oberstleutnant*	*SS-Obersturmbannführer*	lieutenant-colonel
major	*Major*	*SS-Sturmbannführer*	major
captain	*Hauptmann/Rittmeister*	*SS-Hauptsturmführer*	captain
lieutenant	*Oberleutnant*	*SS-Obersturmführer*	lieutenant
2nd lieutenant	*Leutnant*	*SS-Untersturmführer*	junior lieutenant

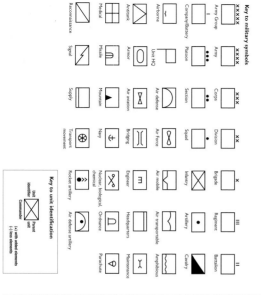

Key to military symbols

xxxxx Army Group	xxxx Army	xxx Corps	xx Division	x Brigade	III Regiment
Army Group	Company/Battery	Platoon	Section	Squad	Infantry
Airborne	Unit HQ				Artillery
Antitank	Armor	Air defense	Air mobile	Air transportable	Cavalry
Medical	Mountain	Air aviation	Air Force		Headquarters
Reconnaissance	Signal	Missile	Navy	Bridging	Ordnance
		Supply		Engineer	Maintenance
				Nuclear, biological, chemical	Amphibious
				Rocket artillery	Parachute
				Air defense artillery	Transport movement

Key to unit identification

Unit identifier
Parent unit
Commander
(+) with added elements
(–) less elements

CONTENTS

INTRODUCTION

To improve upon the greater production times and costs of producing turreted tanks, the Germans mounted main armaments directly into existing chassis, such as the Panther/Jagdpanther and PzKpfw III/Sturmgeschütz III. This late-production Jagdpanther has a bolted mantlet, single driver periscope, and two-piece barrel. The horizontal piece along the lower hull was used to anchor 5mm *Schürzen* plates to provide some protection to the tracks; these plates were designed to prematurely detonate shape-charged rounds, thereby degrading their penetrative capability. A PzKpfw IV L/70 (V) is behind. (Seth Gaines, Aberdeen Proving Grounds)

The road that led to the battlefield employment of the Jagdpanther and the SU-100 in Hungary during early 1945 began in the decade following World War I, when the success of rudimentary French and British armoured vehicles spurred the development of a myriad of vehicle designs, and doctrines on how best to employ the fledgling asset in a future conflict. Most nations viewed these in terms of 'light', 'medium' and 'heavy' based on weight or size, which were indicative of the roles they would undertake in combat. Gone were the evolutionary dead-ends such as the lumbering German A7V 'mobile fortress', and even the more successful, and ubiquitous, lozenge-shaped British Mark series vehicles, which housed the main armament on side sponsons. Throughout the 1930s, experimentation continued, such as with multiple turrets, often to provide vehicles with both HE (high-explosive) and AT (anti-tank) capabilities. Most configurations,

Much as the Germans had developed turretless assault guns that shared a chassis with tanks, that of the ubiquitous Soviet T-34 provided for a variety of vehicles, including the SU-85, SU-122 and SU-100. This is a good illustration of the SU-100's lengthy main armament. Its forward fuel tank port and light bracket (below) are visible on its starboard glacis. An ISU-152 SPG is behind. [Vitaly Kuzmin, Omichi Battle Glory Oblast Museum, Omsk]

however, came to incorporate characteristics that had made the French Renault FT design successful in World War I, such as a single, 360-degree-rotating turret mounting a primary armament, commander's cupola, small crew with a fighting and engine compartment physically separated, and capability to incorporate larger weapons.

Although arms manufacturing matured and expanded to increasingly provide armies with motorized and mechanized elements, the majority of troops remained foot- and horse-bound, and were unable to integrate with, and support, faster-moving armoured formations. One solution was to develop one armoured vehicle type for rapid penetration and exploitation roles, and another for providing slower infantry support. For the Soviets, this manifested itself doctrinally as fast, medium tanks, with integrated mechanized forces for 'shock' operations, and a combination of light 'tankettes' and heavy armour to support a more methodical, broader front. Although the Germans similarly envisaged tanks as part of a mutually supporting group, they preferred to keep them as a separate force to preserve their offensive punch, in which to undertake penetration and exploitation roles. With follow-on, foot-bound infantry requiring armoured assets to help overcome bunkers and built-up positions, in 1935 Oberst Erich von Manstein proposed incorporating *Sturmartillerie* (assault artillery) to fill the gap. Where tanks were well-suited for high-tempo offensive operations, these assault guns eschewed turrets in favour of increased armour protection and larger, more powerful main guns that were mounted into a built-up casemate atop a common chassis.

For the first few years of World War II in Europe, the Heer (German Army) achieved considerable battlefield success, due in large part to its relatively small, but well-led, -trained and -motivated armoured force. While existing German armour and

In response to the Soviet T-34, the Germans developed the Panther, which proved to be an excellent design whose chassis was later used for the Jagdpanther. Here we see a Panther Ausf D (possibly of 5. SS-Panzer-Division *Wiking*) during mid-1944. As the initial model, it was sent into combat at Kursk in July 1943 without adequate testing, and suffered from engine fires and a lack of a bow machine gun. This example sports a drum cupola, turret pistol plug and two mantlet holes for the binocular gunsight. (Nik Cornish @ www.stavka.org.uk)

anti-tank designs proved adequate in the rather limited-distance campaigns in Poland, Western Europe, France and North Africa, the large number of enemy armoured vehicles and seemingly endless spaces encountered during Operation *Barbarossa*, the invasion of the USSR in mid-1941, taxed German capabilities, and – with the release of the newly developed Soviet T-34 medium tank, with its sloped armour, 76.2mm main gun, and excellent mobility and reliability – soon exceeded them. As towed anti-tank weapons, such as the 3.7cm PaK 36, proved little more than a 'doorknocker' against heavier Soviet armour, the Germans resorted to ad hoc solutions, including re-purposing their *Sturmgeschütz* (StuG) assault guns and high-velocity 8.8cm anti-aircraft guns. To help remedy this deficiency, makeshift *Panzerjäger* (tank hunter) vehicles were cobbled together from obsolete domestic and captured foreign designs; their turrets were replaced with a fixed, semi-enclosed shield to protect the crew from bullets and shrapnel, and a more powerful, but limited-traverse, main armament substitute.

Unlike their German adversaries, the Soviets initially failed to see the benefits of turretless vehicles, in part because their utilitarian T-34/76 could be produced in great quantities. Having seen the successful role the German *Sturmartillerie* played in combat, and the lower production costs, the Soviets similarly began development of their own assault guns. Until late 1943, they had only two self-propelled gun options, a 'light,' open-topped SU-76M for engaging enemy AFVs, and the 'medium' SU-122, which was designed to engage softer targets with its howitzer. Both were viewed as mobile artillery, and organized accordingly into mixed regiments to provide integrated support for armoured and mechanized corps. As the war progressed, each side tried to maintain armour superiority; however fleeting; more sophisticated, closed-superstructure Soviet designs based on the T-34/76 and the 'heavy' KV-1 increasingly took the field, and often in such numbers as to rival their fellow tanks.

The Soviets had by 1944 moved to the offensive along the entire Eastern Front, and the lack of a rotating turret made the SPG less suited than the tank to related

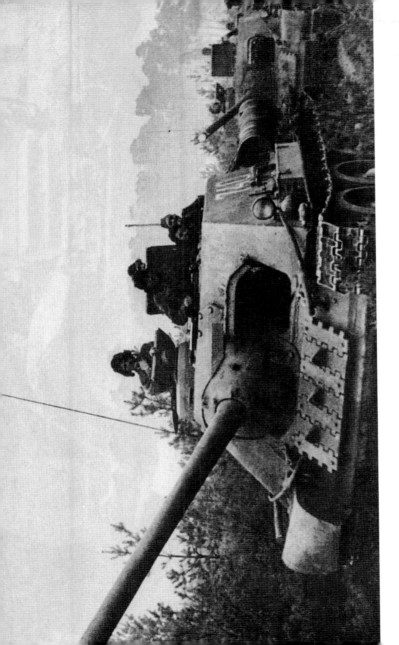

A pair of SU-100s of 1st Ukrainian Front's Thirteenth Army in April 1945. At this time Thirteenth Army had just 1228th Medium SPG Regiment fielding the SU-100. The spare track lengths provided a degree of additional armour protection, while the tow cables were stowed at the ready should vehicle extraction become necessary. The vehicle's 100mm D-10S L/56 main gun was able to damage or destroy most German late-war armour, such as the types encountered in Hungary in 1945. (From the fonds of the RGAKFD, Krasnogorsk via www.stavka.org.uk)

exploitation and pursuit operations. Grouped into batteries, SPGs facilitated an infantry breakthrough into the rear of the opposition's defences either by advancing with the initial assault, or being held back as a reserve, and were only committed once the area to be assaulted had been more fully reconnoitred. Although vehicles such as the ISU-152 served in a heavy tank role during such actions, as its large main armament proved very effective against armoured and reinforced targets, the need to pivot repeatedly in order to engage multiple targets beyond the main gun's traverse risked throwing the tracks or damaging the transmission, and meant such vehicles were better suited to being used defensively. The assault artillery was ill-suited for anti-tank actions in the offensive, although it could engage enemy armour in self-defence or from ambush positions at shorter ranges, using AP shells.

By early 1945, the Soviets had recaptured all the territory lost since Operation *Barbarossa*, the German invasion in mid-1941, and had recently pushed beyond the River Danube in central Hungary. Deficient in men and matériel, the Germans proved unable to resist an adversary that had been steadily supplied with vast amounts of raw materials, food, aircraft and vehicles via Allied Lend-Lease. Faced with impending defeat, and an enemy invasion and occupation of its homeland, Nazi Germany continued to offer resistance, but lacked the strength to stem the tide. With the Red Army having recently overrun Germany's remaining foreign oil production facilities west of Budapest, but now temporarily pausing to prepare for a final, war-winning offensive, Hitler saw an opportunity to get these facilities back, however unrealistic.

CHRONOLOGY

1940

16 January
First Soviet T-34 (A-34) medium tank prototype.

3 March
Germany's first self-propelled anti-tank gun, the Panzerjäger I, is ordered.

1941

22 June
The Germans first encounter the T-34.

25 November
Development of a German medium tank response is ordered.

1942

14 May
MAN's VK 3002 'Panther' prototype is accepted.

3 August
The Germans decide to create a *Jagdpanzer* mounting their new 8.8cm anti-tank gun on a Panther chassis.

1943

17 May
A 'modernized' SU-76M SPG (T-70 chassis) begins trials, and is fielded the following month.

5 July
Panther is first used in combat, at Kursk.

3 August
Jagdpanther development begins.

20 October
First Jagdpanther prototype delivered.

6 November
The ISU-152 assault gun (KV-1 chassis) is adopted as an SU-152 (IS chassis) replacement.

27 December
Development of the SU-100 medium SPG is ordered.

1944

January
MIAG begins producing the Jagdpanther.

March
First SU-100 (Object 138) prototype delivered.

30 July
Jagdpanthers first used in combat, in Normandy, France.

September
SU-100 production begins.

22 September
Having pushed through Romania, the Red Army crosses the Hungarian border.

November
SU-100 is allocated to medium SPG regiments.

As 6. Panzerarmee's commander, SS-Obergruppenführer Josef 'Sepp' Dietrich would be responsible for conducting Operation *Frühlingserwachen*, east of Lake Balaton. Note his World War I badge indicating service with the AFV. Germany's first operational 'tank'. (NARA)

Minimally camouflaged late-model Jagdpanther hulls awaiting assembly at Maschinenfabrik Niedersachsen-Hannover. The gantry crane was used to move heavy loads from the rail line into the factory. Note the small, round air-raid shelter. (NARA)

1945

7 January
SU-100 is first used in combat, west of Budapest, Hungary.

13 February
Budapest falls to the Soviets.

March
Jagdpanther production ceases.

6 March
Operations *Waldteufel*, *Eisbrecher* and *Frühlingserwachen* commence.

9 March
Jagdpanthers of sPzJg Abt 560 engage SU-100s near the village of Dég.

12 March
I. SS-Panzerkorps and I. Kavalleriekorps secure bridgeheads over the Sio Canal. The Soviet 2nd and 3rd Ukrainian Fronts begin their Vienna Offensive.

16 March

1946
March
SU-100 production ceases.

DESIGN AND DEVELOPMENT

JAGDPANTHER

ORIGINS

The Soviet T-34 was first encountered by Axis forces on 22 June 1941, the day Operation *Barbarossa* began, and the German military authorities scrambled to address the threat it presented. Exhibiting a general superiority over the Third Reich's front-line PzKpfw III, IV and 38(t) designs, the 28.5-tonne T-34's performance was hampered by battlefield employment in small, unco-ordinated counter-attacks, minimal crew training and a lack of radios. Even so, over the next few weeks the cumulative effect of such engagements eroded localized German operations, perhaps most famously near the town of Mtsensk on 6 October 1941. As the season's first snow fell, 1 Guards Rifle Corps conducted a well-executed attack with 20 T-34s and several of their 'heavy' KV-1 cousins that ran roughshod over spearheads from the German 2. Panzerarmee moving to envelop Moscow, some 290km to the north. Although they were soon withdrawn to preserve the unit, the onslaught left an impression, and prompted the German commander, Generaloberst Heinz Guderian, to request a special commission to develop a domestic armoured solution.

Early the next month, representatives from the Heereswaffenamt ('Army Weapons Office', or HWA), the Armaments Ministry, armour-manufacturer representatives and designers – collectively making up the Panzerkommission – travelled to the area

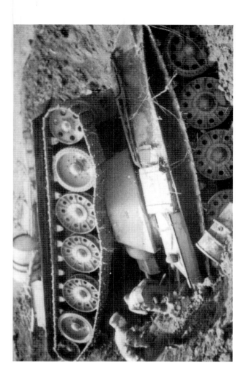

A pair of T-34 Model 1943 tanks that appear to have become victims of an artillery strike. To compensate for rubber shortages, three steel-rimmed road wheels have been incorporated, flanked by quieter rubber-rimmed ones that did less damage to the 550mm plate tracks. Unlike the initial T-34/76 fielded in 1940, this newer version had several improvements, including a roomier 'soft-edge' hexagonal turret, with a smaller vision slit. [NARA]

to inspect captured or destroyed T-34s, and interview their crews. Unlike the multifaceted German vehicles, the Soviet medium tank's streamlined hull provided greater deflection potential and effective thickness, while costing less in labour and material expenditures. Its main gun fired a BR-350A AP, HE round that was sufficient to penetrate all fielded German armour at 1,000m, and its wide tracks imparted impressive manoeuvrability, especially in soft terrain. Although the design suffered from several deficiencies, including poor optics and a two-man turret that made the commander perform double-duty as a gunner and lacked a basket integrating it with the main gun and crew, the Panzerkommission concurred with Guderian's assessment that Germany's own vehicles needed to be improved, and new ones emphasizing larger armament, and improved armour and off-road manoeuvrability should be developed.

On 20 and 25 November respectively, the commission submitted design requirements to Daimler-Benz – one of the firms that had produced the A7V in 1918 – and MAN (Maschinenfabrik Augsburg-Nürnberg AG) for a 30–35-tonne competing design mounting a long 7.5cm KwK 42 L/70 (calibre) main gun. Although MAN was already evaluating a sloped-armour, 24-tonne PzKpfw III/IV replacement that could be easily produced with existing German industrial capabilities, such a vehicle's similarity to the T-34, and need for a new turret, spelled its demise. On 14 May 1942, Hitler approved MAN's heavier, more powerful design, which presented a more conventional German layout that could use an existing turret from Rheinmetall-Borsig, a firm known for its artillery pieces. Although 30–40-tonne AFVs with 532kW engines had been prototyped since mid-1937, the HWA had ordered such efforts halted following the Polish campaign, believing that larger vehicles would not be required for what was anticipated to be a short conflict. With the need apparent by late 1941, the HWA's Heeresabnahmestelle (Army Acceptance Organization', AKA 'Abnahme') subsidiary tasked Waffenprüfamt 6 (Weapons Proving Office (Panzer and Motorized Section), or WaPrüf 6) to co-ordinate vehicle testing and acceptance. In the course of the next year, the personnel who would operate the results of this directive were organized and trained under former Panzerkommission 'tour guide' Mainrad von Lauchert. Although Germany's new Panther Ausf D made an uninspiring, and premature, debut at Kursk in July 1943 – in which its faulty hoses promoted engine fires – the Panther offered an excellent mix of firepower, protection and manoeuvrability that was superior to that enjoyed by its intended rival.

Following the German pattern of modifying existing tank chassis to create a specialized family of vehicles – such as with the *Sturmgeschütz* series, based on the PzKpfw III and IV – on 3 August 1942, WaPrüf 6 decided to mate that of the Panther with a new 71-calibre, 8.8cm high-velocity anti-tank gun. Having worked on a similar effort with Krupp, the department directed this Essen-based armaments firm to undertake the project, which soon determined that considerable modification would

JAGDPANTHER SPECIFICATIONS

General

Production run: January 1944–March 1945 (15 months)

Vehicles produced: 419 (415 delivered + 4 picked up directly)

Combat weight: 45,500kg

Crew: five (commander, gunner, loader, driver, radio/bow MG operator)

Dimensions

Length (hull / overall): 6.93m / 9.654m

Width (without aprons / with aprons): 3.27m / 3.42m

Height: 2.715m

Armour (degrees from vertical)

Glacis (upper / lower): 80mm @ 55° / 60mm @ 55°

Hull side (upper / lower): 45mm @ 30° / 40mm @ 0°

Hull rear (upper / lower): 40mm @ 35° / 40mm @ 25°

Hull roof: 16–25mm @ 83–90°

Hull bottom (front / rear): 30mm @ 0° / 16mm @ 90°

Mantlet: 100mm (Topfblende)

Armament

Main gun: 8.8cm PaK 43/4 L/71 (58 rounds – typically 50 per cent Pzgr 39/43 / 50 per cent Spgr 43; potentially a few Pzgr 40/43 or Gr 39 HL)

Sight: WZF 1/4

Traverse: 24° (12° left/right) (manual)

Elevation: +13° / -8° (manual)

Secondary: 1 × 7.92mm MG 34 (600 rounds); 2 × 9mm MP 40 (24 magazines / 384 rounds); Nahverteidigungswaffe (6 × Nebelkerzen + 10 × 2.6cm Spgr); loosely carried MG (600 rounds)

Main gun rate of fire: 6–10rds/min

Communications

Internal: Bordsprechanlage B intercom

External: FuG 5 10-watt transmitter/USW receiver (wireless telegraphy and radio telephony stationary ranges were 6km and 4km, respectively; an FuG 2 (USW receiver only) was less common, and had a comparable range)

Motive power

Engine: Maybach HL 230 P30 12-cylinder (water cooled) 23.1l (petrol)

Power/to weight: 448kW (sustained) @ 2,500rpm (9.85kW/tonne)

Transmission: Zahnradfabrik AK 7-400; seven forward gears, one reverse gear

Fuel capacity: 720l (in five tanks)

Performance

Ground pressure: 0.89kg/cm²

Maximum speed (road / cross-country): 46km/h / 24km/h

Operational range (road / cross country): 140km / 110km

Fuel consumption (road / cross country): 5.1l/km / 6.5l/km

Fording: 1.55m

Step climbing: 900mm

Climbing angle (up / down): 30° / 40°

Trench crossing: 2.45m

Ground clearance: 560mm

---

be needed. A one-tenth and full-scale model were completed in late September 1942, and on 2 October, orders were issued to produce the vehicle under the lengthy designation 'schweres Sturmgeschütz auf Fahrgestell Panther mit der 8.8cm L/71' ('Heavy Assault Gun on a Panther Chassis with the 8.8 cm L/71'). During a meeting at Minister of Armaments Albert Speer's Reichsministerium für Rüstung und Kriegsproduktion ('Reich Ministry for Equipment and War Production') on 15 October, Daimler-Benz was directed to take over the project, with Krupp focusing on designing the gun and mount. In February it had been decided that an upgraded Panther design was needed, which would share major components with the planned Tiger II, such as tracks, transmission, suspension and road wheels, to improve manufacturing output and maintenance, and reduce costs; the new Jagdpanzer would similarly incorporate such commonality. Due to the limited space at the Daimler-Benz Werk 40 assembly plant in the Berlin suburb of Marienfelde, and problems the firm encountered in meeting production quotas for the Panther, by 24 May it was decided

JAGDPANTHER, sPzJg Abt 560, MARCH 1945

Armour plates would normally be dark grey on their arrival from the armour manufacturer and were primed at the steel works before the final hull assembly. Early Jagdpanthers had interior walls, ceiling and gun components painted Ivory (RAL 1001), with floors in Red Primer (RAL 8012), while vehicles produced after late 1944 commonly had the latter factory-applied to conserve paint and time. Zinc phosphate was the main constituent of the steel primer coats due to their ferrous surfaces; owing to increasing subcontractor decentralization, colour variations occurred.

To provide external camouflage-pattern and colour consistency, in August 1944, factories were required to paint the vehicle. As this consumed production time, a month later, vehicles left the factory in Red Primer

(RAL 8012), with roughly half then being camouflaged by the crews with Dark Yellow (RAL 7028), Olive Green (RAL 6003) and Chocolate Brown (RAL 8017). The vehicle shown here was produced in October 1944, and has these colours applied, in addition to having a small Balkan cross on the superstructure side, and right-side stowage box. Unlike most German AFVs, this Jagdpanther lacks identification numbers.

In November 1944, vehicles were to have an external Olive Green base coat, but this was not universally implemented by war's end. Paint was supplied in 2kg and 20kg paste-like packs, after which it was preferably diluted with petrol prior to use; water could be used instead, but its use made the camouflage susceptible to washing off in rain.

3.27m

2.72m

9.65m

With the teething problems exhibited by the initial Panther Ausf A having been corrected, the Ausf D entered production in August 1943. Its high-velocity 7.5cm main gun, sloped armour and good manoeuvrability made it a well-balanced and effective – albeit somewhat over-engineered – medium tank. Unlike the previous Ausf D model, the Ausf A incorporated a bow machine gun in a blistered housing to provide greater protection against enemy infantry. To better maintain glacis integrity, on the Ausf G model the driver's vision hatch would be eliminated and replaced by a rotating periscope. (NARA)

Unescorted US Eighth Air Force B-17 bombers drop 4lb (1.8kg) AN-M50A2 incendiary bombs over Hannover (probably on 26 July 1943). MNH Linden is circled, while Wülfel and Laatzen are respectively just out of view to the left and bottom. (NARA)

to have Mühlenbau und Industrie Aktiengesellschaft (MIAG) Amme-Werke in Braunschweig produce the vehicle instead. These changes were to be quickly implemented, so that the first hulls could be delivered by the armour manufacturer in September, with the first vehicle to be completed in June 1943 and series production starting the next month.

DEVELOPMENT

Delayed by Allied bombing, MIAG finally presented the first of two *Jagdpanzer* prototypes in October 1943. V 101 was created from the improved Panther Ausf A, in which the front and side armour had simply been extended from the chassis into an enclosed superstructure housing the main gun and crew. The vehicle's streamlined glacis contained the same bow machine-gun port as on the turreted version, a smooth collar mantlet housing the one-piece main gun, and a pair of fixed driver periscopes (one directly forward, and one angled slightly to the left), over which an inverted 'V' protrusion redirected precipitation. Although two rear stowage bins had been fitted to either side of the dual exhaust, it was presently devoid of equipment and affixing components, as well as *Zimmerit*, a concrete-like paste, which had been made mandatory on all German AFVs that month. *Zimmerit* was applied in a lamellar pattern using a toothed spatula to many medium and heavy armour designs and then cured, to prevent the placement of magnetic mines. Three pistol ports were included in the side armour for added visibility (two starboard and one port), and a round opening in the

rear superstructure allowed for loading main rounds and expelling spent shells. During the month Daimler-Benz's full-scale model was transferred to MIAG to aid in completing assembly drawings and procedures, and on 20 October, it was displayed to Hitler at Arys, East Prussia, along with wooden mock-ups of a Tiger II and its *Panzerjäger* equivalent, the Jagdtiger.

The following month, MIAG released their second prototype (V 102), which included welded frames with mountings for entrenching tools, plus a hand winch (thick piece between the exhaust), track tensioner (to its left) and cranking handle (to the right) on the engine deck. The vehicle was to have an MG 34 and two submachine guns stowed inside, and as with all German assault guns and *Panzerjäger*, the Jagdpanther used a roof-protruding periscope for targeting, which was mounted on a plate that could adjust to the main gun's movement. A hatch was included in the superstructure's rear for loading ammunition and performing gun maintenance. Side-opening roof hatches had keyholes for opening, and no handles.

PRODUCTION

Although it had been hoped to begin production in July 1943, continuing delays prompted the creation of two additional facilities to supplement MIAG's efforts: Maschinenfabrik Niedersachsen-Hannover (MNH), and Maschinenbau und Bahnbedarf Aktiengesellschaft (MBA) in Potsdam-Drewitz-Babelsberg. The former, founded in early 1939 to produce armaments, comprised three plants, and upwards of 12,000 employees, mostly Russian prisoners of war. It was headquartered in Hannover-Wülfel (gear wheels and box housings), with subsidiaries in nearby Linden (assembly) and Laatzen (tracks and chassis components); Allied aerial bombing on 28 March 1945 destroyed power and stopped further production. Existing components and chassis continued to be used to construct complete vehicles, however, until Allied forces overran Hannover on 9 April.

Instead of a conventional assembly line, as German heavy industry had previously produced large vehicles such as locomotives, armoured vehicles progressed through a similar construction path comprised of several *Taktzeit* (cycle time) stations where different worker teams added additional components. Hitler designated the vehicle 'Jagdpanther' on 29 November 1943, and it undertook its first demonstration on 17 December, with production finally starting the following month. Optimistically estimated at 150 units per month, in practice a maximum of just 72 per month were built (in January 1945). All told, MIAG built 270 Jagdpanthers (January 1944–April 1945), MNH constructed 112 (November 1944–March 1945) and MBA produced 37 (December 1944–March 1945), for a total of 419.

The early-production Ausf G1 Jagdpanthers were built on the Panther Ausf A chassis, which within a month had the outermost driver's glacis

A late-model Jagdpanther hull (as evidenced by the four upper and lower holes for the mantlet) having its suspension holes bored at one of its *Taktzeit* stations during the production process. (NARA)

vision block removed, and metal welded over the hole. Its 15-tonne rear jack was relocated vertically between the mufflers, and side-mounted vehicle tools and the gun cleaning-rod tube were soon repositioned in the field to the rear engine deck as they could become damaged in wooded areas. This equipment included a thin towing cable, wire-cutters, wood block (just to the rear of the main central hatch), water inlet (left) and fuel inlet (right), hammer, axe, and a small tanker's bar (just forward of the main central hatch), and large tanker's bar (at rear just forward of the cylindrical container for main-gun cleaning rods).

All pistol ports were eliminated in favour of roof-mounted periscopes as the latter did not unnecessarily degrade armour integrity, and modifications incorporated into the new Panther Ausf G were grafted onto the Jagdpanther. Starting in June, the 9.2cm NbK 39 (*Nahverteidigungswaffe*, or 'close-in defence weapon') was integrated into the roof, as were three external Pilze slots for installing a 2-tonne jib crane's legs. Exhaust cooling tubes were fitted to the right engine exhaust pipe starting in July, which reduced the temperature of venting fumes and smoke created by the brake and steering systems.

Although a six-man crew had been proposed on 9 June, the second loader role was eliminated during the production stage, which allowed the number of 8.8cm rounds carried to be increased from 50 to 60. The roof now included hatches for the commander (centre right), the loader (left rear) and a third centred in the superstructure rear, with two fixed and two rotating periscopes. The one-piece gun tube and breech could be removed from the cradle through a large rear hatch after some preparation. To remove its support or transmission, however, the collar had to be unbolted from the frame inside and pulled out through the front.

Starting in May 1944, a two-piece 8.8cm PaK 43/4 L/71 began replacing the monobloc version, as it was made from a 6m-long piece of metal and was more difficult to produce, although the one-piece versions were sometimes used until October 1944. As hand-held weapons, such as the American bazooka or British PIAT, had largely supplanted magnetic mines as the personal anti-tank weapon of choice, *Zimmerit* was discontinued after 7 September, although in partial compensation the factory-applied disruptive camouflage pattern was to be roughly applied. To allow the main gun to be removed through the glacis, a larger mantlet was added, and anchored by four bolts on the top and bottom.

Compared to the early-production Jagdpanthers, those made after December 1944 (designated Ausf G2) had a longer engine deck and shorter, more steeply angled rear superstructure. These vehicles had their exhaust systems enhanced with flame arrestors/suppressors, and units in the field were instructed to install fabricated protective sheet-metal covers from *Schürzen* plates to protect the engine deck's air-intake units. The crew was provided with a heater over the port circular engine vent, and the mantlet's lower section was enlarged. A deflector shield was added just forward of the roof optics and a mounting bracket was positioned on the fifth side skirt at right and left. This final version also received a larger self-cleaning idler wheel, and had its rear shock absorbers, and superstructure stowage bins removed. A few retained the small idler, and had their fighting-compartment exhaust fan mounted over the main gun. There were no Jagdpanther variants, although Krupp worked on mounting the 8.8cm gun on a rear-positioned superstructure, as well as a Jagdpanther II armed with a 12.8cm PaK 80 L/55 gun, but neither was realized before war's end.

SU-100

ORIGINS

At the time of the German invasion in mid-1941, the Soviets had no SPG arm. During the previous decade, experiments had been conducted with such vehicles, but priority production went to turreted tanks as part of Stalin's rearmament programme. The time needed to set up and prepare firing positions and communications was believed to hamper an SPG's battlefield effectiveness. Lighter guns and tanks were to conduct direct fire and act as their own mobile artillery, respectively. The severe tank losses incurred during the second half of 1941, however, spurred Soviet designers to rectify the problem quickly by developing a limited number of standardized designs that incorporated recent hard-won lessons.

Inspired by the reduced production costs and versatility of the German *Sturmgeschütz*, the Soviets fielded an interim solution that placed the 76.2mm anti-tank gun on the hull of a T-70 light tank – the SU-76M. Although it became the Red Army's most numerous SPG, the type's thin armour and semi-enclosed crew area made it unsuited for cold-weather and urban-combat environments. As the SPG concept proved its worth on the battlefield, the Soviets, like their adversaries, progressed to heavier designs – a capacity they would have greatly lacked were it not for matériel and expertise provided by foreign companies during the 1930s. In January 1940, the Soviet T-34 medium tank prototype began testing, with production slated for September. Had the Soviets waited for an improved T-34M to be fielded, prototypes would not have been available until March 1941, and production would have made little impact after the German invasion three months later.

As the 'inferior' version proved more than a match for its German contemporaries, the T-34/76's chassis was a logical choice to house a 122mm M-30 howitzer. Fielded in December 1942, the SU-122 proved an adequate solution for its intended infantry-support role, but its low rate of fire and limited traverse made it unsuited for engaging moving targets. To address this shortcoming, within a year, the Soviets produced a more purpose-built tank hunter incorporating the same 85mm main armament as on the improved T-34. Like the German 8.8cm piece, the D-5S gun had been converted from an anti-aircraft gun due to its high muzzle velocity, but by the time it was fielded in the SU-85, it was inadequate against heavier German tanks, such as the Panther and Tiger I, not to mention redundant.

Having concluded that the SU-85 could not structurally withstand the recoil from a longer 122mm or 152mm main gun – the installation of which would necessitate several labour-increasing structural changes, add 3 tonnes to the vehicle, and limit the incorporation of new technologies –

A German StuG III Ausf E platoon command vehicle, as demonstrated by its two antennas. At just over 2m in height, its low silhouette proved advantageous as it presented a smaller target, and allowed for greater armour and firepower than those enjoyed by its tank equivalents; these were qualities the Soviets would seek to match in the form of SPGs based upon their T-70, T-34 and KV-1 chassis. The flag was used for aerial friend-or-foe identification. (NARA)

on 11 November 1943, Soviet designers agreed to incorporate a 100mm piece instead. 46 days later, the Soviet National Defence Committee (GKO or 'Gosudarstvennyj komitet oborony')[1] issued decree no. 4851 to incorporate the weapon (later changed to 122mm) into a new tank IS-2 design, based on the KV-1 chassis and named the 'Iosef Stalin'. On 28 December 1943, the People's Commissariat of the Tank Industry of the USSR (NKTP or 'Narkomtiazhprom'), an organization created on 11 September 1941 to oversee all Soviet armoured vehicle manufacturing, issued order no. 765. This tasked the Ural Heavy Machinery Factory (UTZM or 'Uralmashzavod') with mass-producing the new SPG prototype, as the factory had pre-war experience building large mining and metallurgical-related machines, and more recently the T-34, and its SU-122 and SU-85 derivatives.

DEVELOPMENT

Given a first-stage development timeline of just 18 days in which to produce an SU-85 replacement prototype, Chief Designer L.I. Gorlitskiy, heading a team of leading experts including N.V. Kurin (chief engineer) and V.L. Likhomanov (electrical), initially considered using a converted D-34 naval gun, but tests conducted at Gorokhovets in early January 1944 indicated it would require too much effort to convert it to land use, and it – and a D-10-85 – were rejected. As the BS-3 field gun had nearly the same dimensions as the D-5S, which largely negated costly adjustments, and was effective against the Panther and Tiger I beyond 1,500m, and the Ferdinand Panzerjäger at up to 2,000m if against its side, Plant No. 9 soon began producing it instead as the D-10, with postwar designations of 'T' (tank), or 'S' (self-propelled gun). Although suitable 100mm HE ammunition was plentiful, supplies of AP rounds were not expected until after mid-1944.

1 The National Defence Committee had Stalin as chairman. This tightly controlled, very centralized network of lower-level party and industrial leaders had been instituted a week after the German invasion, and had overriding control of local governments with respect to military, industrial and economic issues.

A good physical comparison between an SU-100 (left) and an SU-85 (right) outside UTZM. Besides the noticeable difference in gun sizes, the SU-100 has the same cupola used on the T-34/85. (From the fonds of the RGAKFD, Krasnogorsk via www.stavka.org.uk)

The T-34/85 – shown here in the foreground, with a T-44 and an IS-2 behind it – made the SU-85 essentially redundant, and prompted the fielding of the up-gunned SU-100. Here, spare track links provide additional protection for the glacis; the cupola is identical to those of the transition SU-85M and the SU-100. (Vitaly Kuzmin, Central Museum of the Great Patriotic War 1941–1945 in Moscow)

With UTZM having assigned its Factory No. 9's design bureau, under F.F. Petrov, to undertake actual development of the SU-100 project, work progressed quickly. Between 20 and 25 February 1944, the 'Object 138' prototype passed its second phase of testing, which at UTZM Plant No. 50 in Yaroslavl, fired the main gun 30 times, and operated for 150km without significant issues. A week later the vehicle was sent to the Gorokhovets artillery range for its third, and final, testing stage. Between 9 and 27 March, 'Object 138' was successfully subjected to 1,040 firings and 864km of operation, and the Commission deemed it could be incorporated into the Red Army after making some minor changes, including adding an electric trigger lock to the main gun to prevent unintended firing, replacing gas/oil crankshaft lubrication with oil only, and improving the commander's position, latch hatches, tool and ammunition stowage, and superstructure ventilation. Until the SU-100 became operational, Gorlitskiy championed an interim solution that had UTZM use an 85mm D-5S-85 main gun, which imparted a 20 per cent increase in penetration. This was designated the SU-85M (Modernized) and on 14 April 1944 they began preparations for mass-producing the SU-100, which were completed on 5 May. In modifying the S-34 for vehicle use, Plant No. 9 reduced the cradle's width to 160mm and added new traverse and elevation mechanisms, and a new gunsight.

From 24 to 28 June the SU-100 fired 923 test rounds, this time against captured tanks and SPGs, including a Tiger I, a Panther and a Ferdinand, the heavily armed and armoured SPG developed from Ferdinand Porsche's Tiger I chassis. Using newly provided AP UBR-412 rounds, its 100mm main gun penetrated the glacis of the first two vehicles at 1,500m, but not the third. Although these results were promising, similar outcomes would be unlikely to be achieved in a combat environment.

PRODUCTION

To save costs and manufacturing time, all of the SU-100's major components remained unchanged from the SU-85, including the engine, transmission and chassis, which meant that just 16.5 per cent of the vehicle was created from scratch, in this case installation components to mount the new main armament. The remainder came from existing vehicles, including the T-34 (72 per cent),

SU-100 SPECIFICATIONS

General

Production run: September 1944–March 1946 (18 months)

Vehicles produced: 3,037 (initial run) (1,350 through to April 1945)

Combat weight: 31,600kg

Crew: four (commander, gunner, loader/radio operator, driver)

Dimensions

Length (hull / overall): 6.1m / 9.45m

Width: 3m

Height: 2.25m

Armour (degrees from vertical)

Glacis (upper / lower): 75mm @ 50° / 45mm @ 55°

Hull side (upper / lower): 45mm @ 40° / 45mm @ 0°

Hull rear (upper / lower): 45mm @ 48° / 45mm @ 45°

Hull roof: 20mm @ 90°

Hull bottom: 20mm @ 90°

Mantlet: 40–75mm

Casemate side: 45mm @ 0–20°

Casemate rear: 45mm @ 0°

Casemate roof: 20mm @ 90°

Armament

Main gun: 100mm D-10S L/56 (33 rounds in total; typically 22 OF-412 (HE), 11 BR-412/BR-412B (APHE-T))

Sight: TSh-19 articulated telescope (4×); MK.IV periscope

Traverse: 16° (8° left/right) (manual)

Elevation: +20° / -3° (manual)

Secondary: 3 × PPSh-41 submachine guns

Main gun rate of fire: 6rds/min

Communications

Internal: TPU-4-BisF intercom

External: 10-RT-26 10-watt transmitter/10-RF-26 receiver, with stationary and moving ranges of 24km and 16km, respectively

Motive power

Engine: 12-cylinder (water cooled) 38.88l (diesel/petrol) (V-2-34)

Power/to weight: 298kW (sustained) @ 1,700rpm (9.5kW/tonne)

Transmission: Constant-mesh; five forward gears, one reverse gear

Fuel capacity: 670l (400l + 4 × 90l external tanks (3 fuel + 1 oil)

Performance

Ground pressure: 0.8kg/cm²

Maximum speed (road / cross-country): 50km/h / 20km/h

Operational range (road / cross-country): 200km (310km with external fuel tanks) / 140km (215km)

Fuel consumption (road / cross-country): 2.1l/km / 3l/km

Fording: 1.3m

Step climbing: 730mm

Climbing angle: 35°

Trench crossing: 2.5m

Ground clearance: 400mm

SU-122 (4 per cent) and SU-85 (7.5 per cent). As the 100mm gun extended further forward than its predecessor, overloaded front rollers were strengthened by increasing the diameter of the wire springs from 30mm to 34mm. After final modifications, on 3 July GKO decree no. 6131 officially cleared the SU-100 for Red Army service, although for the next several weeks, UTZM produced it in parallel with the SU-85M.

In September 1944, a few pre-production SU-100s were sent for front-line testing, where their manoeuvrability and increased firepower elicited praise from their crews. Since the 100mm BR-412B ammunition would not become available until October, most production SU-100s were temporarily relegated to military schools or training facilities. Once supplies of the AP rounds began shipping to the front on 11 November, vehicles were sent into combat the following month. Not long after it was fielded, the notoriously poor ventilation the SU-100 initially shared with other Soviet AFVs was largely rectified by the inclusion of two roof-mounted fans, with bell-shaped covers. No wartime variant of the SU-100 was developed.

SU-100, 382nd GUARDS MEDIUM SPG REGIMENT, MARCH 1945

As with other Soviet armoured vehicles, SU-100s such as the one shown here tended to be painted in an overall dark Protective Green 4B0, although there was some variety from light to black green. Two-colour camouflage schemes of contrasting greens, dark earth or ground brown were rare, as were three-colour varieties of green, dark earth and yellow, or red. During the winter vehicles could be painted with washable Type B white paint.

Geometric and numerical markings presented a compromise between security and organization, as the Soviets refrained from using standardized tactical markings. When used these consisted of between two and four digits, or a combination of two numbers or geometric signs. With local commanders commonly issuing tactical numbers, the "310" on this SU-100 probably indicates the battery and vehicle. Other than this, this vehicle's regiment used no other markings.

Additional identification could be painted on the vehicle's roof and sides for aerial identification, such as after 24 April 1945, when white crosses were applied during the fight for Berlin; from 1 May, white triangles were used. White, yellow or red patriotic slogans or fundraiser acknowledgements were often painted on the superstructure sides, such as *Za Rodinu* ['For the Motherland'], or *Za Stalina* ['For Stalin']. Although a Guards emblem was often applied, national varieties were seldom displayed.

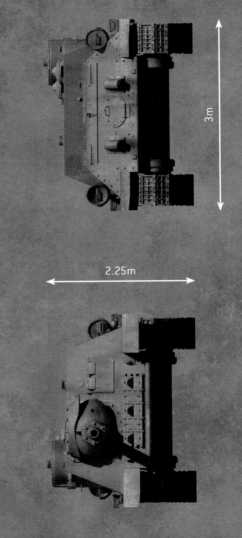

3m

2.25m

9.45m

TECHNICAL SPECIFICATIONS

ARMOUR

JAGDPANTHER

Starting on 5 January 1943, Daimler-Benz personnel met in Berlin to define the various technical issues related to producing what was now called the '8.8 cm Sturmgeschütz auf Panther', and would continue to do so for the next four months.

On 1 May, the Heereswaffenamt specified the vehicle's armour shape and thickness for the renamed '8.8 cm Panzerjäger 43/3 L/71 auf Panther Fahrgestell', which was to be commensurate with the proposed up-armoured and up-gunned Panther II – although the project was discontinued three days later, in favour of focusing on mass-producing the original. By 1943 the escalating Soviet and German race for tank and anti-tank superiority, however fleeting, translated into ever-larger vehicles, with greater firepower and armour. With armour up to 80mm thick, the depth negated the use of face hardening, a process commonly applied to strengthen early-war plate by stiffening the outer layer to deflect or shatter an incoming round, while retaining flexibility on the interior to diffuse its impact energy and retain structural integrity.

Produced by Brandenburgische Eisenwerk Kirchmöser, based in Brandenburg an der Havel, the Jagdpanther's rolled homogeneous armour (RHA) began as cast ingots, which were infused with various enhancing elements, such as small amounts of nickel

A Jagdpanther of sPzJg Abt 654 near Remagen, Germany, on 1 April 1945. Wires cover the superstructure and barrel to affix camouflaging foliage. A field-applied Olive Green (RAL 6003) is visible over its factory-applied Red Primer (RAL 8012) base coat. (NARA)

and molybdenum for hardness, and chromium for resistance to corrosion, oxidation and abrasion. As Germany was forced to relinquish territory after 1942, stockpiles of these components dwindled. Substitutes, such as vanadium, were used as grain-growth inhibitors to improve the steel's toughness, although malleability commensurately suffered. As RHA's strength came from having a consistent hardness throughout, variations during production promoted stress-concentration boundaries that reduced ballistic resistance, and to compensate, German designers accepted an increased armour thickness that might not otherwise have been needed.

As production was frequently disrupted by Allied bombing, the tempering process of repeatedly heating the raw metal to 800°C, and cooling it in water or oil, could not always be done with the accuracy required to produce optimal alloyed-steel plate. As a result of this 'scale effect' a crystalline microstructure (collectively called bainite) could form internally, which increased hardness and the potential for impact cracking. In contrast with US equivalents, German plates suffered from hydrogen embrittlement, a metallurgical condition, which reduced ductility. Subsequently, an impacting projectile's shockwave would be increasingly likely to produce a dangerous internal showering of metal flakes known as spall.

To test finished lots of RHA, a 5cm uncapped Pzgr 39 AP round would be fired against an 80mm plate, and if a crack did not form the plate would be passed for assembly. The Jagdpanther had a Brinell Hardness Number (BNH) (a standard metallurgical test to determine impact characteristics based on a unit of force) of between 250 and 290; higher numbers indicate harder/more brittle metal, while lower numbers indicate softer/more malleable metal, and most AFVs of the period fell between 200 and 450. In combat, the vehicle's upper glacis tended to be more susceptible to cracking (due to its large area), as compared to the more resilient lower portion, as illustrated by Allied tests showing that US 90mm and British 17-pdr APCBC projectiles would not penetrate an un-cracked Panther glacis, even at extremely short range. If the glacis was already cracked, however, subsequent rounds were much more likely to achieve penetration.

Although 15mm floor plates were common in German *Panzerjäger*, an additional 10mm was included in front to protect the driver and radio operator from mine damage. 5mm-thick *Schürzen* plates along the side resisted or disrupted the penetrative power of shape-charged weapons against the tracks or suspension components. The Jagdpanther's 100mm-thick *Topfblende* (pot mantlet) provided an excellent design that eliminated the shot trap on earlier models of the StuG III, and comprised a relatively soft, molybdenum-free steel casting bolted to the upper glacis for easier dismounting.

JAGDPANTHER FIGHTING COMPARTMENT

The Jagdpanther's interior layout was similar to other German AFVs, with the driver and radio-operator/machine-gunner in front, the commander, gunner and loader in the central fighting compartment, and the engine in the rear. The driver sat on a leather-cushioned seat that could recline horizontally, and used the same instrument panel as on the Panther. Unlike most German armoured vehicles, the Jagdpanther had steering levers extending down from a cross bar, which made them awkward and taxing to use for extended periods. Its mechanism attached to both the support and hydraulic-assisted disc brakes, under which the driver's clutch, brake and accelerator resided, while a gear shift and release hook were affixed to the transmission housing.

Clamps for a gas-mask canister, breathing tube and fire extinguisher were also readily available. Although his periscope was on the same level as the main gun, which assisted hull-down manoeuvring, without its mate, the driver's view was very restricted, and he relied heavily on directions from the commander and other crew-members. The commander was positioned behind the radio-operator, who doubled as the bow machine-gunner, on the starboard side of the main gun, where he was provided with a rotating scissor-type SF 14Z periscope. The gunner was positioned on the port side of the main gun, across from the commander, while the loader worked at the rear of the fighting compartment, where two seats were provided, one on either side of the breech.

1. 8.8cm PaK 43/3
2. Mantlet
3. Bow machine gun
4. Radio operator's seat
5. Commander's seat
6. Radio
7. 8.8cm rounds
8. Loader's seat
9. Breech
10. Spent-round hole
11. Loader's seat
12. Drive shaft linkage
13. Gun foundation
14. Gunner's seat
15. Elevation wheel
16. Driver's seat
17. Periscope

SU-100 FIGHTING COMPARTMENT

The driver occupied the vehicle's front, and was provided with a glacis escape hatch with two prismatic vision ports that made for easy evacuation, and a torsion mechanism to facilitate opening and closing; this hatch weakened the vehicle's frontal armour, however. A speedometer and tachometer, intercom port, starter button and electric panel were to the driver's left. The clutch, brake and fuel pedals were on the floor, with a pair of compressed-air cylinders above the latter as a starter backup should electrical power be lost. A lever to his left and another to his right protruded from the floor and controlled turning, while the control panel and illumination light were

positioned below the glacis hatch. A 160-litre fuel tank and eight 100mm rounds were to his right. The remaining three crewmen worked within the SU-100's central fighting compartment, alongside 25 rounds of 100mm ammunition, divided into five sections. The commander's position had a cupola, with five vision slits in which vertically sliding interior blocks could be raised to position armoured glass over the opening to provide visual protection, and lowered when not in use. The cupola also had a roof-mounted MK.IV periscope, which was situated to the right of the main gun, with an emergency exit hatch under the commander's seat.

1. Gunner's seat
2. Loader's seat
3. Clutch pedal (brake and circular fuel pedals to the right)
4. Control lever
5. Instrument panel: clock, oil temperature (in and out) and oil pressure
6. Access hatch, with vision port
7. Revolver hole port
8. TPU-4-BisF intercom
9. MK.IV periscope
10. TSh-19 gunsight
11. Traverse wheel
12. Elevation wheel
13. Breech
14. Commander's seat
15. Ventilation units
16. Commander's cupola
17. 100mm D-10S

This view of an SU-100 shows its bolted mantlet (similar to that of the Jagdpanther), firing port (between the driver's hatch and the roof-mounted MK IV periscope) and a bolt below each tow hook for adjusting track tension via the idle wheel. Soon after the Soviet SU-100 had been introduced to combat in Hungary and East Prussia in January 1945, the Germans captured a few examples. One was sent off for testing, where the German experts concluded that only the new super-heavy tank 'Maus' being developed would be entirely immune to the Soviet 100mm gun's AP rounds. Recently deployed heavy armour such as the Tiger II was resistant to such projectiles only across its frontal arc. (Vitaly Kuzmin, Central Museum of the Great Patriotic War 1941–1945 in Moscow)

SU-100

Although striving to provide armour with a hard outer face to reflect as much energy as possible and dissipate the remainder over a large area while providing a ductile interior that resisted deformation and spalling, Soviet armour designers balanced these desires against existing manufacturing technology, and mass-production efficiency. As the majority of incoming projectiles would be across the SU-100's frontal arc, a 75mm-thick glacis angled at 50 degrees proved sufficient at resisting most impacts encountered on the battlefield. By relying on flat, angled armoured slabs, the hull and superstructure incorporated RHA, which had greater ballistic strength due to its having been worked and shaped to align the grain structure. Although RHA was common by mid-1944, production costs increased due to the tempering process involved with creating thicker plates, but these fabricated sections were then welded which – if done correctly – did not unduly compromise the plate's metallurgical characteristics.

To increase production numbers – and keep costs low, considering the overhead of expanding complex, expensive milling facilities and the resulting extra steps involved in production – the SU-100 incorporated cast armour as much as possible. By simply pouring molten metal into a mould a variety of shapes could be created, such as the cupola or mantlet. Once cooled, external imperfections, such as 'gate marks' where the molten metal entered the cavity, were removed before carrying out a tempering process of heating the metal above its critical temperature, then allowing it to air-cool. Because of contemporary manufacturing technologies and techniques, Soviet cast armour suffered from inconsistent thicknesses. Internal flaws due to improper heat treatment or the use of low-quality alloys were also common, which with the substitution of manganese for nickel resulted in a hard, high-carbon finished product, especially along the weld seams. Unlike RHA, the grain structure was not modified, and was therefore not as strong, or impact-resistant, although the overall curved shape exposed less exterior surface area for the equivalent volume, which better distributed stress and resisted glancing rounds. In general, cast armour was hard, but it was also more prone to shattering. Although higher-quality Lend/Lease US steel was becoming more available, an attempt was made to harden the armour using tempering, but this meant an increase in production times and cost. Where the KV-1 averaged a relatively soft 250 BHN, later Soviet armour was a harder 400–450, which being over the 375 'machineable' designation meant it could not be cut with standard factory cutting tools.

Two tow hooks were welded to the lower front and rear plates, while rails, brackets, external fuel/oil tanks and accessories were affixed to the hull, with mud flaps added along the fender sides. Spare-parts boxes were fixed to shelves on the left front and right rear, the engine compartment was protected by an armoured box, and a spare section of track was commonly affixed to the glacis for added protection. Three hatches provided access to the internal oil tank, and the suspension's fourth and fifth rollers, while one in the floor provided for crew escape.

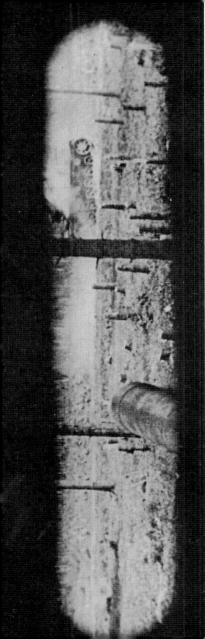

ARMAMENT

JAGDPANTHER

Tasked on 1 July 1942 with developing a new 8.8cm anti-tank gun, Krupp opted for an entirely new KwK 43 L/71 design, while their Rheinmetall-Borsig competitor simply forwarded a re-worked Flak 41 L/74 anti-aircraft piece. As the former was shorter, possessed a muzzle brake and used smaller, more easily stored projectiles, the Heereswaffenamt agreed to its production. In February 1943, the cruciform mount was designated the PaK 43, followed by a series of guns: PaK 43/41 (two-wheel split-trail carriage), PaK 43/1 (Nashorn), PaK 43/2 (Ferdinand/Elefant), PaK 43/3 and 43/4 (Jagdpanther) and KwK 43 (Tiger II). This was initially developed as a monobloc barrel, but the considerable internal pressure and stress produced by firing high-velocity rounds necessitated a change to a two-piece variety. This eased construction and changing barrels, which needed to occur after 2,000 firings – or 1,200 when using the Pzgr 39-1 round.

Early Jagdpanther sights were the same Sfl Zf 1a 5×8 periscopes (*Selbstfahrlafetten-Zielfernrohr*, or 'self-propelled telescopic sight') as were fitted on the Ferdinand/Elefant, while later versions used the WZF 1/4 (*Winkelzielfernrohr*, or 'angled telescopic sight'). A linkage enabled the sight to traverse with the main gun, and eliminated the need for a large roof opening as with previous *Sturmgeschütz* designs.

To the transmission's starboard side, the radio-operator/hull machine-gunner worked the 7.92mm MG 34 anchored within a glacis *Kugelblende* (ball mount) via a rubber handle grip, and trigger. Its integrated KgZF 2, 1.75× monocular sight to the left provided an 18-degree field of view; its reticle had no range or deflection settings, but zeroing adjustments were provided, as was illumination. A face pad offered protection during viewing, and a head pad was used for depressing the gun, which was affixed with a balance spring that tended to pull the gun toward the upper left during sustained firing, and a travel lock. The MG 34 theoretically fired a blistering 850 rounds per minute from belts stored in 150-round canvas bags, and although this

Inside a Jagdpanther. Here, the top shelf holds a *Fernhörer* (remote handset), while 'Füllung bei 6 'Erfg braun.ark' indicates the recoil cylinder needs to be filled with a high-viscosity oil suitable for arctic temperatures when employed in cold-weather environments. The right-hand crewman is wearing protective coverings for his forearms, and is likely to be the loader. The crewman behind the breech isn't in a position, but judging by his *Gefreiter* sleeve patch, he would be the radio operator. (NARA)

SU-100

The fixed 100mm BR-412 (БР-412) APHE-T round (**1**) comprised a 65g RDX-based main charge (A-IX-2) to assist in penetration, a base-detonating MD-8 (МД-8) fuse, and a No. 7 tracer for ensuring detonation and improving targeting visibility. A pair of copper driving bands helped seal the round inside the gun chamber and prevented propellant gases from escaping, which would degrade velocity. Its bulging ogive, and deep grooves, promoted integrity during impact. Weighing 30.1kg, its rather heavy 15.88kg projectile made it less susceptible to crosswinds. The text on the round reads: 'ПОЛНЫЙ' ("fixed"), 'УБР-412' (brand), '100 – 44' (calibre – year),

"СУ-100 И ТАНК" (for SU-100 or tank use), "НДТ-3 18/1 38/D 0" (propellant data), "1-0-00" (lot number), "Ф" (fragmentation).

The 30.2kg (15.6kg projectile) 0F-412 HE round (**2**) used 1,460g of Trotyl (70 per cent tetryl/30 per cent TNT) as an explosive. An RGM (point-detonating) fuse set off the 15.6kg projectile, which was effective against hard and soft targets. The text on the round reads: 'T' (Trotyl), 'ПОЛНЫЙ' ("fixed"), 'УОФ-412' (brand), '100 – 44' (calibre – year), 'СУ-100 И ТАНК' (for SU-100 or tank use), 'НДТ-3 18/1 38/D 0' (propellant data), '1-0-00' (lot number), 'Ф' (fragmentation).

JAGDPANTHER

The APCBC/HE-T Pzgr Patr 39/43 [**3**] – *Panzergranatepatrone* or 'armour grenade cartridge', modified in 1943 from a 1939 design – was the Jagdpanther's primary AT round. Specifically designed to handle the high internal barrel pressures within the PaK 43 L/71 gun, the projectile possessed a tracer and a second driving band for added stability and accuracy over its Pzgr 39-1 predecessor (which could still be used, provided the main gun had fired fewer than 500 times). Its hard shell was capped by softer metal to minimize disintegration from high-velocity strikes, while the addition of a ballistic cap reduced drag. It also caused enemy armour to crack and weaken before the shell made contact, and promoted better penetration, after which the shell's Amatol (60 per cent TNT/40 per cent ammonium nitrate) bursting charge would explode. The projectile could also be used by other 8.8cm guns, as indicated by the text on the cartridge ('8,8cmStuK43/1'; '8,8cmStuK43'; '8,8cmStuK43/1'; '8,8cmPak43'; '8,8cmPak43/41'). The text on the cartridge also gives the weight (6,900kg); the explosive charge ('GuRP-G1,5-(725/650-5,1/2)' – where 'Gu' indicates Gudol propellant, 'RP' indicates tube sticks, 'G1,5' indicates the propellant's caloric efficiency and '(725/650-5,1/2)' indicates the tube length and thickness); the manufacturer and manufacture date of the fuse ('dbg1943/1', where 'dbg' indicates Dynamit AG); and the manufacturing location and date of the round ('Jg20.1.43K').

The HE Sprgr Patr 43 [**4**] – *Sprenggranatpatrone* or 'explosive grenade cartridge', a 1943 design – was used against unarmoured vehicles, infantry and static defensive positions. The projectile had no tracer, and except for a second driving band it was the same as the older L/4.7 version. It relied on Amatol explosive; as per the Pzgr Patr 39/43, the projectile could also be used by other 8.8cm guns as shown by the text on the cartridge. The text on the shell indicates where and when the fuse was manufactured ('14 Jg20.1.43'); the round's weight class ('III'); explosive ('R8'); and the round's manufacturing location and date ('Jg18.1.43N'). The tip (firing pin and nose) and the

piece extending into the round was the AZ 23/28 (*Aufschlagzünder* or 'impact fuse'), around which was the main explosive filling. This fuse type could be set for direct-action or delay; it was so sensitive that tank crews were warned against firing through trees or other obstructions just beyond the barrel for fear of premature detonation.

The Gr Patr 39/43 HI [**5**] – *Granatepatrone 39/43 Hohlladung* or 'grenade cartridge 39/43 hollow charge', modified in 1943 from a 1939 design – was a HEAT projectile that relied on a shaped charge to penetrate armoured vehicles. Again, the projectile could also be used by other 8.8cm guns as indicated by the text on the cartridge. The text on the shell indicates the kind of round ('HI'); cyclonite/wax explosive ('91'); the fuse manufacturer and date ('Jg20.1.43'); the weight class ('III'), and the round manufacturer and date ('Jg18.1.43N'). The round's tip comprised a small direct-action AZ 38 fuse, which on impact detonated a conventional hollow charge that was set back to allow the conical liner and explosive to properly form a high-velocity metal jet. The rear component is the detonator. As only about 7,000 shape-charged Gr Patr 39/43 HI rounds were produced, their use was uncommon, and the round's low velocity and degraded effectiveness from having to spin made it suspect with many crews.

The Pzgr Patr 40/43 [**6**] – an HVAP/-T round, modified in 1943 from a 1940 design – was to be used against the thickest enemy armour. The limited availability of tungsten after 1943 meant that the 'HK' (*Hartkern* or 'hard core') Pzgr 40/43 AP composite rigid projectile was also produced with steel ('S' for *Stahlkern*) or iron ('W' for *Weicheisen*) core expedients. The all-black round acted as a kinetic penetrator and had a smaller explosive charge than the Pzgr Patr 39/43. Because of its lighter weight the shell was affected by wind resistance and decreased accuracy. Compared to the production of 1.98 million Pzgr Patr 39/43s and 2.48 million Sprgr Patr 43s, only about 5,800 Pzgr Patr 40/43s were made. (German ammunition views by Jim Laurier, ©Osprey Publishing)

cyclic rate could be increased using spring-assisted drums, they held fewer rounds. Generally, two ammunition bags were positioned under the weapon: one to feed it from the left, and one to collect the empty shell casings at the right. The MG 34's wooden butt, sights and bipod mount were stored in a wooden box to allow it to be used outside the vehicle if necessary. The elevation and traverse arcs of the bow machine gun were some 27 and 30 degrees respectively.

For close-proximity defence, the Jagdpanther was equipped with a 9.2cm *Nahverteidigungswaffe* (close-in support weapon), which extended through the roof at 39 degrees, and could have smokescreen-producing Schnellnebelkerze 39 or Rauchsichtzeichen canisters fired through it. For protecting external 'dead space', a Sprenggranatpatrone (HE) could be used, which had a 7–10m range, and a one-second fuse designed to detonate 0.5–2m above the ground.

SU-100

The 100mm Model 1944 D-10S 56-calibre main gun weighed 1,435kg, and was mounted in the SU-100's glacis via bolts. With the hull opening protected by a curved mantlet, internally the horizontal sliding breech block recoiled up to 570mm; being semi-automatic, it returned to its forward position with an open breech for the next round. The gun possessed recuperator and hydraulic buffers, and had a primary electric trigger backed by a hand-operated mechanical device. It used an articulated TSh-19 gunsight that provided 4× magnification.

Like the SU-85, the SU-100 had no integrated secondary machine gun, as the vehicles were expected to operate as support, or alongside covering infantry or aircraft, and not act independently. For crew defence, the fighting compartment officially contained two 7.62mm PPSh-41 submachine guns with 1,420 rounds of ammunition (20 drum magazines), four AT grenades and 24 F-1 hand grenades. A pair of rear-mounted TDP smoke systems was fitted to the vehicle's rear, which launched MDSh canisters via two dashboard toggle switches to provide a localized smoke screen.

MOBILITY

JAGDPANTHER

To avoid production delays and to maximize vehicle hardware interchangeability, it was decided to use the HL 230 P 30 (*Hochleistungsmotor*) engine. Built by Maybach, Auto Union (four automobile manufacturers, including Audi) and Daimler-Benz, it was being used in Germany's other heavy AFVs, including the Panther and late-model Tiger I. Jagdpanthers were fitted with a ZF AK 7-200 (later a strengthened ZF AK 7-400) transmission, which, being a synchromesh variety, utilized a cone clutch and blocking ring to transition smoothly between gears rotating at different speeds. Using air drawn from the outside, circular, grate and mesh-covered fans forced cooling air out of the radiator bays on each side of the engine. The Maybach power plant was a water-cooled petrol engine, and required a large radiator area to maintain a proper operating temperature. The swirling cyclone action of the air around these holes forced larger dirt and dust particles to the outside edges where they fell out of the filter box. The vehicle's 23.88-litre engine was rated at 522kW at 3,000rpm, but actually delivered a more reasonable 485kW at 2,500rpm.

Although the Jagdpanther was physically lower, cheaper and quicker to manufacture than the Panther, its weight and speed were marginally worse. The vehicle had MAN single-radius controlled differential, steering levers, mechanical disc brakes and an 8.7m turning radius. Eight interleaved, independently sprung twin steel-rimmed, rubber-cushioned road wheels per side were fitted; these improved maintenance and cold-weather operation as ice and snow were less likely to impede rotation. A double torsion-bar suspension offered the best support for the 45,000kg vehicle, with swing arms acting forward (port) and rearward (starboard). This provided independent wheel movement in the vertical, increased stiffness in turns, helped retain stability over rough terrain, and permitted a theoretical maximum speed of 46km/h, although this was not recommended during general operation. Each rod traversed the hull, having entered at a round bearing, crossed to the other side and attached to a pivot. The bars passed through two hull supports running the vehicle's length that acted as braces for the transmission and seats, and the bearing points were lubricated via a tangle of oil lines. The Jagdpanther had a 17-tooth front drive sprocket, an adjustable rear idler,

Pictured near Altenkirchen, some 35km north-east of Remagen, Germany in late March 1945, this Jagdpanther has been flipped over by an aerial bomb, offering a view of the road-wheel arrangement. The vehicle's double torsion-bar suspension provided a relatively smooth ride, and its interleaved wheel arrangement helped distribute its weight, but at the cost of additional maintenance when needed. (NARA)

An SU-100, with rubber-rimmed road wheels. The protrusions behind the cupola are ventilation fan covers. (Vitaly Kuzmin, Omichi Battle Glory Oblast Museum, Omsk)

one return roller per track, and shock absorbers on the second and seventh road wheels. Each 660mm-wide, 2,050kg dual centre-guide steel track had 86 shoes.

SU-100

The SU-100's power plant and transmission were identical to those of the T-34/85, except for housing modifications. Its 12-cylinder, four-stroke diesel engine was rated at 336kW at 1,700rpm, although sustained output was closer to 298kW, with a maximum 373kW at 1,800rpm. A pair of air cleaners used cyclone action to provide flow to the engine cylinders. The V-2-34 engine used 'DT' type diesel, as well as 'E' type (OST 8842) petrol. 400 litres of fuel were carried internally along the vehicle's sides, and connected to the engine using an NK-1 pump, while 80 litres of oil circulated through the system via a three-section gear pump. On either side of the engine, two tubular radiators provided cooling.

The rear-mounted transmission consisted of a multi-disc clutch, with a manual five-speed gearbox (with constant mesh gears), multiple-disc steering clutches (steering clutch brake), and final drives. A 1kW GT-4563A generator and four rechargeable 6-STE-128 A\h batteries provided electrical power, including 12V (lighting) and 24V (starting), and powered various components, including two MV-12 ventilation fans, the main gun's trigger, radio and internal intercom. Should this fail due to mechanical problems or cold temperatures, a backup starter relying on one of two compressed-air canisters was available.

To compensate for an increase of 30mm of glacis armour over that of the T-34, and its lengthy 100mm gun, the SU-100's front suspension was strengthened. It had Christie-type coil spring-loaded torsion arms that each supported five 830mm-diameter, independent, rubber-rimmed alloy double wheels per side. Power was directed through rear-mounted double sprocket wheels, which worked in conjunction with track-tensioning front idler in front. Cast-alloy steel, dry, loose-pin cast-manganese tracks comprised 72 500mm-wide cast-steel links, with alternating 172mm central guides. Each track weighed 1,150kg and had an expected service life of 1,000km.

THE STRATEGIC SITUATION

THE SOVIET JUGGERNAUT

In early 1945 the military situation facing Hitler's regime was bleak indeed. Since conducting amphibious landings in France and Italy, US, British and Allied forces had pushed across North West Europe to the borders of Germany, during which time the Jagdpanther had its successful battlefield debut. With a surprise thrust through the heavily forested Ardennes region having proved successful against France four years earlier, Hitler hoped to repeat the undertaking on 16 December 1944, thereby securing Antwerp and effectively dividing the Allied forces. Within a week, though, the offensive had been checked, and by mid-January 1945 the German 'bulge' had been eliminated, and the Allies were rekindling their push eastwards.

In the East, where the Heer maintained roughly half its strength, the Red Army had moved to the operational offensive. On 22 June 1944, in commemoration of the day the Germans invaded the USSR three years earlier, the Red Army had commenced Operation *Bagration*, which in just under a month effectively eliminated the German Heeresgruppe Mitte (Army Group Centre) and overran Byelorussia. Between 20 and 29 August, the Soviet 1st and 2nd Ukrainian fronts destroyed much of Generaloberst Johannes Friessner's Heeresgruppe Süd Ukraine (South Ukraine). As Red Army efforts to press into the Carpathian Mountains and Bulgaria progressed, German reserves were moved from the primary Warsaw–Berlin axis of advance; the Soviets encircled and

Following the Allied penetration of the Westwall and crossing of the River Rur, on 25 February the US 899th Tank Destroyer Battalion pushed through Düren, Germany, and past this knocked-out, late-production Jagdpanther Ausf G2 of sPz.Jg Abt 564. Note the impacts in the glacis, starboard track and mantlet. (NARA)

Along the lengthy Eastern Front, vast quantities of Allied Lend-Lease matériel, foodstuffs and transport had enabled Soviet forces to fight a war of mobility and logistics, against which their depleted German adversary could not effectively respond. Captured and repurposed by the Germans as an observation post, this American-built M4A2(76)W Sherman, with steel track chevrons, was one of 2,073 76mm-armed Shermans provided to the Red Army via Lend-Lease. During the fighting between Budapest and Vienna in early 1945, they would be used by I Guards Mechanized and V Guards Cavalry Corps. (NARA)

destroyed much of General der Artillerie Maximilian Fretter-Pico's 6. Armee and forced Heeresgruppe Süd Ukraine's shattered 8. Armee, under General der Infanterie Otto Wöhler, to withdraw westwards into Hungary. Following Romania's surrender and occupation by the Soviets on 12 September, the entire southern sector of Germany's Eastern Front was made untenable. Over the next few weeks, the inexorable Red Army drive steadily overran parts of Czechoslovakia, Yugoslavia and Hungary east of the Danube, forcing Hitler to relinquish the Balkans. Understanding the political significance of Red Army gains in South East Europe, British Prime Minister Winston Churchill visited Stalin in October to define zones of control. The Soviet Premier agreed to leave Greece to the British; three-quarters of Hungary, however, was to be controlled by the Soviets, mostly as they had already overrun much of the country, and were moving on the capital, Budapest.

In South East Europe, Germany's senior leaders planned to maintain a defensive stance everywhere except Hungary, where in the coming year they would focus on securing a north–south front line that included Budapest. Hitler saw Hungary as the first line of defence surrounding the industrial region around Vienna and southern Germany, and in late 1944 and early 1945 he commensurately attached great political and military importance to retaining his remaining ally. With the loss of Romania's oil fields, only Zisterdorf, near Vienna, and Nagykanizsa, at Lake Balaton's south-western edge in Hungary, remained available, along with what synthetic fuel plants remained in Germany. In strengthening central Hungary's defences, Hitler seemed unconcerned with stabilizing other fronts, especially before Berlin. Instead of husbanding his remaining forces for national defence, and the chance of an armistice – a remote possibility considering the Western Allies' stipulation of accepting unconditional surrender only – he would remain focused on continuing the war, and salvaging remaining German-controlled assets and territory.

HUNGARY'S DILEMMA

In 1940, Hungary had joined the so-called Tripartite Pact, the German–Italian–Japanese alliance system, and over the next few years participated in subduing Yugoslavia, and later the fighting in the USSR. As the war continued, however, many of Hungary's conservative leaders – including Miklós Horthy, who had taken control of the country in 1920 as regent – were quietly manoeuvring to limit their commitment to Germany. By March 1944, with the Soviets threatening Hungary's eastern border, the Hungarian Prime Minister, Miklós Kállay, had been discussing an armistice with the Western Allies for over a year – a situation that kept American and British bombers from striking Budapest.

The aristocratic Miklós Horthy rose to become commander of the k.u.k Kriegsmarine (Austro-Hungarian Navy) at the end of World War I. Between 1919 and 1921, he led ultra-nationalist forces in a repressive campaign to eliminate Hungary's communist elements once their revolutionary government had been ousted. Horthy subsequently established himself as the nation's leader, a position he held until 1944. (Public domain)

Informed by intelligence of the Hungarians' plans, Hitler invited Horthy to the palace of Klessheim, outside Salzburg, on 15 March to conduct 'negotiations'. With the Hungarian military temporarily deprived of leadership, German forces initiated a 'protective measure', by quickly occupying the country, and secured its important industrial facilities as part of Operation *Margarethe I*, four days later. With seemingly no option save compliance, on Horthy's return to Budapest the new authorities informed him that the country would remain sovereign only if he removed Kállay and established a more co-operative government. As the alternative meant a German-appointed *Gauleiter* who would treat Hungary as an occupied enemy country, Horthy appointed Döme Sztójay as prime minister. The initial plan had been to immobilize the *Honvédség* (Hungarian Army), but with Soviet forces having overrun Bulgaria and Romania before moving on Hungary from the north, east and south-east, the Hungarians decided to retain their forces centrally, and to send a contingent to defend the Carpathian mountain passes to the north.

On 15 October, Horthy announced an armistice with the USSR; this was largely ignored by his armed forces, which continued to fight against what they saw as an invading foreign power. The next day, the Germans responded with Operation *Panzerfaust*, which in concert with Honvédség elements secured Buda Castle, important public buildings and rail facilities in the capital, and detained Miklós Horthy, Jr. This final act forced the detainee's father to abrogate any moves toward an armistice and depose the newly created 'government', naming the leader of the far-right Arrow Cross Party, Ferenc Szálasi, as prime minister of a new German-controlled 'Government of National Unity'.

STALIN MOVES ON BUDAPEST

To capitalize on Soviet momentum, Stalin was adamant that Budapest be taken as soon as possible to promote Hungary's subjugation, berating Marshal Radion Y. Malinovsky, the 2nd Ukrainian Front commander, with 'I categorically order you to begin the offensive on Budapest tomorrow.' With much reservation, on 29 October, Malinovsky sent his depleted armies attacking westwards from bridgeheads that had been established across the River Tisza in central Hungary, towards their prize, some 90km away. In the vanguard of 600,000 Soviet and 35,000 Romanian soldiers, 750 armoured vehicles and 1,100 aircraft, Forty-Sixth Army was tasked with taking the capital.

The opposing Axis forces had been conducting a fighting withdrawal for two months, with minimal resupply or replacements, and Heeresgruppe Süd Ukraine was in poor shape. Roughly 350,000 German and 150,000 Hungarian defenders awaited the inevitable, and although they fielded some 500 tanks and assault guns, there was a critical deficiency in artillery numbers. Fretter-Pico pulled his men back to shorter, more defensible positions south of the Hungarian capital, organizing surplus manpower into reserves to counter enemy efforts more flexibly. Already several days behind Stalin's schedule, between 11 and 15 November, Malinovsky pushed ahead some 40km to keep 2nd Ukrainian Front from getting bogged down in attritional fighting. Faced with losing Budapest, on 1 December Hitler designated it a *Festung* (fortress), in which the city, like others in similar instances, was to be defended to the last, and thereby tie down a disproportionate number of the enemy.

Having taken Belgrade in early December, 3rd Ukrainian Front, under Marshal Fyodor Tolbukhin, reached the Danube to the south of Malinovsky's forces. Now with adequate resources, on 19 December the 625,000-strong 2nd Ukrainian Front thrust westwards just north of the River Danube bend, while 3rd Ukrainian Front's 450,000 spread from Yugoslavia to south of Budapest. With the Soviets soon securing bridgeheads over the Danube near Lake Balaton, Fretter-Pico quickly withdrew to establish a new defensive position known as the 'Margarethe Line'; within a week, however, Soviet forces penetrated deep into the Axis rear, taking the strategic city of Székesfehérvár on Lake Velence to anchor the 3rd Ukrainian Front's left flank as its armoured spearheads turned north to envelop Budapest. On 26 December, Forty-Sixth Army spearheads triumphantly linked up with friendly forces in the Danube bend to effect the encirclement of the Hungarian capital.

The 31,583 soldiers of SS-*Obergruppenführer* Karl von Pfeffer-Wildenbruch's IX. SS-Gebirgskorps were now trapped in Budapest, along with some 1,500 Heer personnel and 87 AFVs; 37,000 Hungarian soldiers offered support. By 1 January 1945, the focus of German efforts changed to lifting the siege and stabilizing the front along the Danube, which would enable them to redirect formations north to defend Poland, and prevent the Soviets from concentrating on Berlin. By this time the Pest defenders east of the Danube had been pushed into a steadily constricted perimeter, while those in Buda had remained relatively static. Intent on relieving the beleaguered city, the Germans launched Operation *Konrad* that night, deciding upon a direct attack over the hilly, heavily wooded terrain of the Transdanubian Mountains north-west of Budapest. Waffen-SS armoured forces penetrated the overextended Soviet Fourth Guards Army near Tata, and threatened to push into Forty-Sixth Army's inner ring. By 3 January, the Germans had penetrated some 40km – roughly halfway to their destination – and Tolbukhin, commander of the outer encirclement ring, was forced to rush four corps from around Székesfehérvár to buttress his crumbling line. Malinovsky, commanding the inner encirclement ring, pulled a rifle corps from his fight and redirected it to assist, halting the German relief force at Bicske, just 25km from the capital.

Hosök tere ('Heroes' Square') in downtown Budapest depicts leaders of the seven tribes that founded Hungary in 896, and other notable historical figures. Atop the 36m column, a statue of Archangel Gabriel holds the crown of Hungary's first king, Stephen I, while at its base is the Tomb of the Unknown Soldier. (Magdi Gulyas)

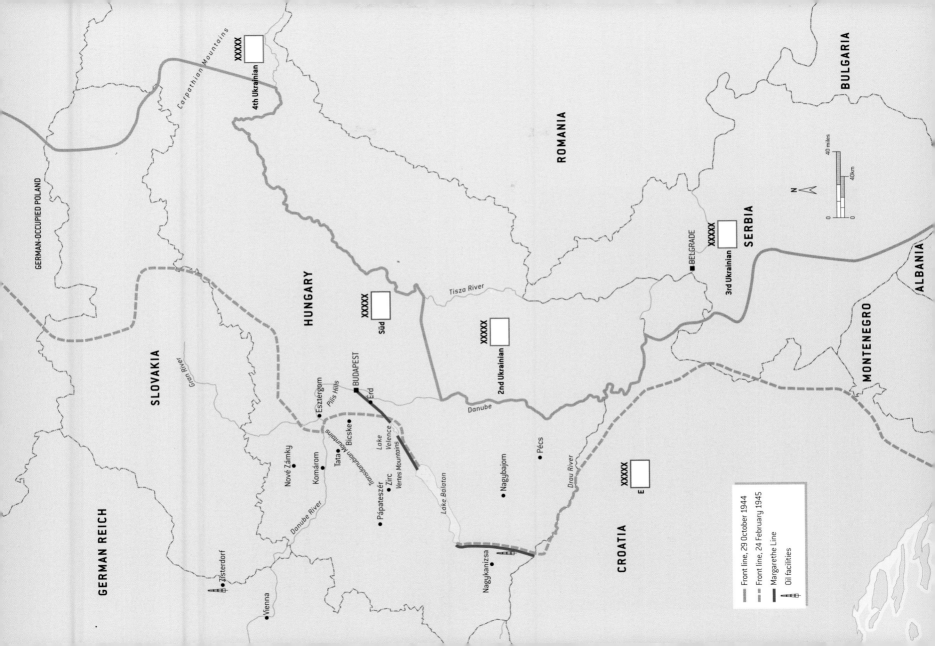

GERMAN-OCCUPIED POLAND

BULGARIA

ROMANIA

Carpathian Mountains

XXXXX
4th Ukrainian

SERBIA

XXXXX
3rd Ukrainian

■BELGRADE

Tisza River

HUNGARY

XXXX
Süd

XXXXX
2nd Ukrainian

SLOVAKIA

Gran River

MONTENEGRO

ALBANIA

N

40 miles

40 km

Esztergom

Pilis Hills

BUDAPEST
Érd

Danube

Nové Zámky

Komárom

Tata

Bicske

Transdanubian Mountains

Zirc

Pápateszér

Vértes Mountains

Lake
Velence

Pécs

Nagybajom

Drau River

XXXXX
E

Danube River

GERMAN REICH

Zisterdorf

Vienna

Lake Balaton

Nagykanizsa

CROATIA

Front line, 29 October 1944
Front line, 24 February 1945
Margarethe Line
Oil facilities

Introduced into Soviet service in mid-1943, the SU-152 was nicknamed 'Big Game Hunter' due to its ability to damage or destroy heavier German armoured vehicles, which were named for various animals. Although its 152mm howitzer had a low rate of fire and velocity, the kinetic energy generated by its HEAT rounds could simply smash that armour it did not penetrate. Developed on the KV-1's chassis, the SU-152 had 60–75mm upper-glacis armour that was sufficient for its intended assault gun role, but only carried 20 rounds for the main gun. This example was commanded by a Lieutenant Karakudov and served with 2nd Baltic Front. (Courtesy of the Central Museum of the Armed Forces Moscow via www.stavka.org.uk)

Simultaneously, on 6 January Malinovsky's premier armoured formation, Sixth Guards Tank Army, smashed a 15km hole in the Axis positions north of the Danube near Esztergom, and during the next three days pushed 80km towards the major Axis supply hub at Komárom. To facilitate the Soviet effort, three SU-100-equipped units – 382nd Guards, 1453rd and 1821st medium SPG regiments, serving with I Guards Mechanized Corps – were introduced into the fighting. By 7 January, the Budapest garrison was steadily pushed towards the city centre as the Axis supply situation became critical. In a follow-up attempt to reach their besieged comrades, SS-Obergruppenführer und General der Waffen-SS Herbert O. Gille's IV. SS-Panzerkorps sent 3. SS-Panzer-Division *Totenkopf* into the attack just south of Esztergom at 2030hrs on 10 January. Fighting against the weather as much as time, Gille managed good progress over the Pilis Hills. As I. Kavalleriekorps, with sSS-Pz Abt 503 in support, had drawn Soviet forces toward its sector north-west of Lake Velence, *Totenkopf's* forward elements advanced to where they could communicate via flares with the Budapest garrison. With success seemingly in sight and looking for a more substantial victory, on 11 January Hitler ordered Gille to pull out of the Danube bend and head south. Despite its success, the German relief force, overextended and vulnerable, was unable to exploit this small breakthrough. The defenders of 'Festung Budapest' refrained from breaking out, even though such a course now had the best chance of success.

In a third, and final, effort to raise the Budapest siege, Gille attacked Soviet supply convoys and artillery positions on 18 January, reaching the Danube by the morning of 20 January, and pushing north into Fifty-Seventh Army's rear, threatening it with encirclement. Four days later, *Totenkopf* and 5. SS-Panzer-Division *Wiking* went into the breach yet again, inflicting heavy losses on the Soviet V Guards Cavalry and I Guards Mechanized Corps, until finally being stopped 24km south of Budapest. Pulling back to a defensive position between Lake Balaton and Lake Velence,

IV. SS-Panzerkorps regrouped in preparation for an offensive in Hungary. For the next two weeks, 'Festung Budapest' held out, but at dawn on 12 February, thousands of German and Hungarian personnel attempted a breakout through the wooded hills north-west of Budapest, as their military role in the Hungarian capital was no longer of value. Budapest fell the following day.

HITLER'S RESPONSE

As Seventh Guards Army's extended position along the Danube's northern bank threatened to be a springboard for a Soviet thrust on Vienna, on 17 February the Germans initiated Operation *Südwind* to eliminate it. Since 6. Panzerarmee had pulled out of the Ardennes sector Soviet intelligence had failed to determine its movements accurately. Speculating it would be transferred to Berlin's defence, or at least central Germany, the Soviets were surprised when the Panzer army suddenly appeared in the Budapest sector. Using some 400 armoured vehicles, Dietrich's command, with support from two tank battalions from 2nd Hungarian Armoured Division, struck the unsuspecting Seventh Guards Army, which fell back. 1. SS-Panzer-Division *Leibstandarte-SS Adolf Hitler* and 12. SS-Panzer-Division *Hitlerjugend* pressed ahead on a 16km frontage, across terrain crisscrossed by numerous canals; after an advance of some 8km, they encountered several anti-tank guns and dug-in T-34/85 tanks. Armoured battle groups from both divisions advanced on 19 February, employing Tiger II and Panthers in leading-wedge formations to present their thicker frontal armour to the threat, and by early afternoon German elements reached the Danube.

The next day, 6. Panzerarmee's advance continued with a push northwards to counter IV Guards Mechanized Corps, still entrenched on the west bank of the River Gran. Additional attacks to the south during the night of 22/23 February resulted in German blue-on-blue casualties, but by the next day, I. SS-Panzerkorps prepared for the final assault on the Soviet bridgehead. *Leibstandarte* and *Hitlerjugend* initiated a concentric night attack, which forced the defenders to withdraw over the Gran's remaining bridge before blowing it up at 0830hrs on 24 February. The Soviets left a considerable amount of destroyed and abandoned armour, artillery and equipment, and suffered more than 2,000 killed, 6,000 wounded and 500 captured. In comparison, the Waffen-SS formations sustained some 3,000 casualties, plus a dozen tanks destroyed and many more damaged.

For six weeks, 72,000 German and Hungarian defenders had tied up almost 500,000 Soviet troops, and although the time gained provided the Axis forces a brief respite in which to reorganize, the fighting resulted in some 76,000 Hungarian civilian, 16,500 Honvédség and 47,000 German casualties. In contrast, Soviet killed, wounded and missing amounted to roughly 320,000, which rivalled the 352,000 losses that would be incurred during their subsequent offensive to capture Berlin ten weeks later. Horthy's continued calls for a truce had little impact on Honvédség soldiers, and most continued to fight alongside the Germans. With Heeresgruppe Süd – as Heeresgruppe Süd Ukraine was now known – crippled, the path to Vienna, Czechoslovakia and the southern border of Germany was exposed to yet another, possibly final, Soviet offensive.

THE COMBATANTS

TRAINING AND ETHOS

GERMAN

Throughout the war, most German training was conducted through the Ersatzheer (Replacement Army). Special courses were also used to develop a pool of trained personnel as possible officers and NCOs. By late 1944 wartime shortages, and the need to field soldiers quickly, meant that *Grundausbildung* (basic training) was commonly reduced from 16 weeks to just eight, and comprised individual, squad and platoon

After treatment in the field and at the battalion aid station, a wounded German soldier would be sent 6–8km back to a main clearing station for any initial surgery or short-term recovery. Note the skull emblem on the sign and the Adler W61K mudguard, indicating a facility of 3. SS-Panzer-Division *Totenkopf*. (NARA)

training segments. *Erweiterungsausbildung* (advanced training) followed, usually until the trainee was transferred to the field, and focused on small-arms and close-combat skills, physical fitness, sports, lectures and drill. A variety of *Waffenschulen* (weaponry schools) provided instruction in equipment, weapons, and tactics related to specific services such as engineers, artillery and armour, while also creating instructors.

For tanks and SPGs, personnel with mechanical or technical skills were naturally most desired, with training conducted at one of several armour facilities including Grafenwöhr (Germany) and Oldebroek (Netherlands). Although each crewman was to become familiar with the others' duties, the interaction between the commander, loader and gunner was particularly stressed, as their close co-operation translated into rapid battlefield responses. Because enlisted and officer candidates participated in training together, the sense of comradeship between the two groups was correspondingly strengthened. Unlike the Waffen-SS, where there was a more relaxed atmosphere between officers and lower ranks, the Army instilled a distinct separation between the two.

Casualty evacuation focused on the immediate sorting of the wounded to determine injury severity, with those lightly injured to get back to duty as quickly as possible, and the remainder to rapidly get appropriate medical attention. If wounded the soldier would initially be carried or walk to his respective battalion *Verwundetennest* (aid station), which was located as close to the front as practical, and provided first aid and stabilization for those needing to be sent to the regimental *Truppenverbandplatz* (aid station) some 500m to the rear. Wounded categorized as ambulatory were directed rearward on foot, or if unable were sent to an ambulance loading post, and then to a *Hauptverbandplatz* (main clearing station). Seriously wounded personnel would then be sent to local field hospitals or permanent facilities at home.

SOVIET

Starting on 23 April 1943, self-propelled formations moved from the artillery branch to the Red Army's armoured and mechanized forces. This change also meant that the

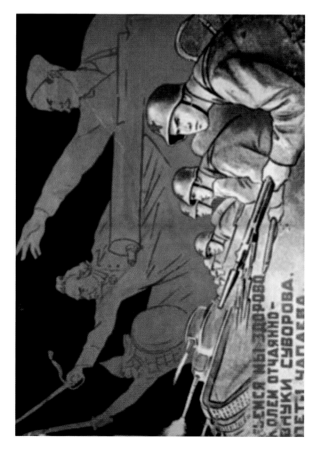

Both sides used propaganda that stressed that the present fight was akin to those of their ancestors or historic heroes, in this case stating: 'We are fighting very well, grandsons of [Alexander] Suvorov, children of [Vasily] Chapaev'. These men were, respectively, an 18th-century Imperial Russian Army generalissimo who purportedly never lost a battle, and a World War I veteran and Bolshevik martyr of the Russian Civil War. [Public domain]

2nd Kiev and 2nd Rostov Self-Propelled Training Schools and the 18th, 19th and 21st Self-Propelled Training Regiments – and their related personnel and warehouses – were similarly re-categorized, with new recruits and officers now allocated from the armoured depots.

Although the SU-100 was a roughly finished, unergonomic vehicle, its powerful main gun and good armour protection and manoeuvrability made it well liked by its crews, especially those moving from the SU-85. The vehicle commander tended to be a lieutenant, with the remaining crewmen being sergeants. NCOs received roughly three months of training that comprised specialized class work and training on the SU-100; this focused on loading, aiming and firing the main gun, ammunition care, radio operation, and technical and mechanical skills. Additional training involved tactical procedures, negotiating a variety of natural and constructed terrain types and obstructions, and – about a third of the time – night manoeuvres, as well as driver training. Most of the cadets possessed little, if any, armoured combat experience. The new units were then transported to reserve-status training brigades and regiments behind the front lines, before finally being sent into combat. As with their late-war German counterparts, morale was supported by nationalist and political rhetoric, although many Soviet commanders retained a mindset that assumed tactical deficiencies could be compensated for by employment en masse, strong discipline and the acceptance of high casualty levels.

Soviet medical care was rudimentary, with each higher echelon being responsible for evacuating its subordinate units' casualties. To help ensure wounds were quickly addressed, casualties were treated at nearby mobile battalion aid stations, where a pair of doctors were posted. Mobile therapeutic field hospitals tended to those with less serious injuries. The medical system was based on several stages of increasing distance from the front, which depended on the wound's type and severity, and the immediate military situation. Medical supplies and procedures were generally insufficient and outdated; antibiotics were scarce, and morphine more so. Individuals in platoons were supplementarily trained as medics in addition to their combat duties. As few Soviet soldiers had received preventative typhus, tetanus, malaria, cholera and other inoculations – unlike the personnel of Western armies – illnesses in the Red Army were common, and the Red Army's medical corps' efforts to isolate and evacuate contagion cases were not always successful in containing outbreaks.

ORGANIZATION

GERMAN

The Jagdpanther entered service in April 1944. The turretless *Sturmgeschütze* had been fielded in concert with traditional tanks since 1940; the descendant *Panzerjäger* varieties had by now come to the fore, and in some instances supplanted them. To make the best use of the relatively limited number of such vehicles, they were optimally to be organized into independent 45-vehicle battalions, as stipulated in their official *Kriegsstärkenachweisungen* (table of organization) from 1 March 1944. With exceptions for research, training and piecemeal allocations, these formations were allocated to corps- and army-level commands, where they were allocated as 'fire brigades' or mobile reserves to help shore up threatened sectors.

Schwere Panzerjäger-Abteilung 'Panther' (numbers of Jagdpanthers in parentheses)

HQ staff and staff company (3, with additional radios)

Three companies, each with company HQ troop (2), plus three platoons (4 each)

Signals, engineer, anti-aircraft and workshop platoons

Supply company

SOVIET

The Soviet SU (*Samokhodnaya Ustanovka*, or 'self-propelled mounting') regiments were categorized as light, medium and heavy organizations, although distinctions varied over the war's course. Replacing the SU-85 with the SU-100 in existing medium SPG regiments began in November 1944, with an amended organizational structure No. 010/462 that stipulated 382 personnel and 21 SU-100s plus support units. As more vehicles were provided, starting the following month, brigades were formed from three medium SPG regiments. Including commensurate support elements, each was to contain 1,492 personnel, 65 SU-100s and three SU-76Ms for reconnaissance.

Medium SPG brigade (numbers of SU-100s in parentheses)

Brigade HQ, including a control company (2) and a reconnaissance company (3 SU-76M)

Three medium SPG regiments, each with regimental HQ (1) and four SU-100 batteries (5 each), plus submachine-gun company, engineer platoon and rear units

Anti-aircraft machine-gun company

Counter-espionage section 'SMERSh'

Rear units, including a technical support company

DOCTRINE AND TACTICS

GERMAN

As prescribed by the Inspekteur der Panzertruppen (Inspector General of Armoured Troops), Generaloberst Heinz Guderian, on 14 June 1944, the Jagdpanther's primary responsibility was to employ its 8.8cm main gun to destroy enemy armour at long range. If several targets presented themselves, it was recommended to engage them quickly, and at ranges of 2,500m if possible – while if hidden, the Jagdpanther crew were to let enemy vehicles run across their fire front. Frequent changes of position and firing from unexpected directions enhanced results. Soft targets, such as infantry or transports, were secondary and only valid in the absence of enemy armour, or if other German heavy weapons were unavailable and sufficient Jagdpanther ammunition existed.

The 42mm×60mm Panzerkampfabzeichen (Panzer Assault Badge) in bronze was instituted on 1 June 1940 for Panzer personnel who participated in three different armoured assaults on different days (a silver version had been produced since 20 December 1939 for AFV crews and units). It depicted an early-model PzKpfw IV surrounded by oak-leaf wreath. Starting on 22 June 1943, it was issued with engagement denominations of grades II ('25'), III ('50') and IV ('75' and '100'). (Public domain)

HERMANN BIX

Hermann Bix (10 October 1914–31 July 1986) was born in Gross Strehlitz, near the Silesian capital of Breslau. He became a machinist after leaving school, and later applied for service in Germany's interwar 100,000-man Reichswehr, but was declined. Undaunted, he joined the Heer soon after its formation in May 1935, and by October that year was serving with Pz Rgt 2 in Eisenach. After serving as a motorcyclist with Pz Rgt 35 during the Polish and French campaigns, by the start of Operation *Barbarossa* he had risen to tank commander in 7./Pz Rgt 35. Under his battalion commander, Major Lauchert, Bix was credited with destroying 60 enemy vehicles, 12 anti-tank guns and 16 artillery pieces, and capturing over 800 prisoners, for which he was granted the Iron Cross First Class. After switching to 6./Pz Rgt 35 on 1 October 1941, he participated in 2. Panzerarmee's advance on Tula, during which he captured a Soviet petrol warehouse intact, which serviced the division. As he continued towards Mtsensk, he was caught up in 4th Tank Brigade's counter-attack with KV-1s and T-34s. During the German operational withdrawal from Moscow several weeks later, in which much Axis equipment needed to be abandoned, he served as an infantryman.

Allocated to 8./Pz Rgt 15 the following spring as a platoon commander, he was wounded in an arm and a leg by a shell splinter on 30 June, but remained with his unit, until wounded again on 22 August when his mount struck a mine. Sent to a German hospital on 5 November 1942, he was awarded the German Cross, and following his recovery took a position as Academic Director of the Heeresunteroffiziersschule (Army NCO School) in Eisenach.

Having served in this capacity until spring 1944, Bix was made an instructor in a Panzer division in France that had just received its first Panthers. In June, he was transferred back to the Eastern Front, where he fought at Warsaw and the Kurland Peninsula. Fighting in a Jagdpanther, he was wounded twice more, but remained with his unit, and on 25 February 1945 destroyed 16 enemy armoured vehicles. On 7 March, he participated in his division's breakthrough towards Danzig. As part of a Jagdpanther platoon, Bix supported operations near Stargard in Pomerania where he knocked out four American Lend-Lease tanks. Over the next two weeks, he destroyed a further 11 armoured vehicles, and was awarded the Knight's Cross by radio on 22 March 1945. Wounded for the final time on 6 May, he was evacuated across the Baltic Sea to Kiel, which surrendered to the British just over a week later. Discharged from captivity at year's end, he joined the postwar Bundeswehr in 1956, eventually retiring in 1970. Credited with the destruction of 75 enemy armoured vehicles, Bix died in Wiesbaden in 1986.

Hermann Bix. (Public domain)

The vehicle's manoeuvrability made it suited to lead mobile operations, although it was to avoid fighting in restricted terrain, or without infantry support, due to its limited visibility. The Jagdpanther was not to be used as a static towed anti-tank weapon, or as self-propelled artillery, and after fulfilling its combat mission, it was to be withdrawn to the battalion workshop platoon for restoring combat readiness. Each *schwere Panzerjäger-Abteilung* was preferably to be employed as a unit to maximize combat effectiveness, and minimize supply and command-and-control problems. If individual companies had to be used, they needed to be directly attached to units smaller than a division. Platoons were only to engage fortified positions and in difficult terrain, while individual Jagdpanthers were expressly to avoid action. Although they could be used to reinforce anti-tank defences, where they could be utilized against an enemy's main thrust, it was inappropriate to use them to secure positions.

ALEXANDER N. KIBIZOV

Like Bix, Alexander Kibizov (27 October 1912 – 29 March 2001) did not participate in the fighting in Hungary, but his career is indicative of the combat experiences of many veterans of both sides all along the Eastern Front. Born to a peasant family in North Ossetia along the Georgian border, after graduating from junior high school Kibizov was drafted into the Red Army in August 1942. He served as an infantryman west of Moscow, where he was soon wounded. In April 1943, he returned to the front as a sergeant, and commander of an SU-122 as part of 1454th Medium SPG Regiment. Having fought at Kursk, he was awarded the Order of the Great Patriotic War Second Class, for the courage and bravery he displayed. On 4 November 1943, he served with 1445th Regiment, IX Mechanized Corps near Kiev, where his platoon destroyed a withdrawing enemy motorcade, earning him the Order of the Red Banner. Throughout 1944, Kibizov moved across the western Ukraine between Kiev and the River Bug, before continuing across the 1939 Soviet/German border, and over the River Vistula.

In March 1945, Kibizov was transferred north to Pomerania, and on 16–17 April fought at the Seelow Heights, some 60km from Berlin. Now an SU-100 commander in 1454th Medium SPG Regiment, as part of First Guards Tank Army, he acted as his regiment's vanguard; he destroyed five enemy tanks and three anti-tank gun positions. On 22 April, he was one of the first Soviet soldiers to enter the German capital, where he fought his final actions north of the village of Karlshorst, and covered friendly infantry crossing the River Spree into the centre of the city.

At war's end, Kibizov's kill tally included 24 armoured vehicles, 62 trucks and APCs and 28 artillery guns. 'For courage and heroism in the offensive operations of the Vistula to the Oder, and causing great damage to the enemy in manpower', on 31 May 1945, he was given the Hero of the Soviet Union and the Order of Lenin. After the war, he lived in Kislovodsk in the North Caucasus, and managed a hospital until retiring in 1980. Five years later, Kibizov moved to the North Ossetian capital of Vladikavkaz, where he died in 2001.

Alexander N. Kibizov. (Public domain)

When attacking, as accuracy at slow speeds was little better than at higher speeds, it was directed that movement be carried out as quickly as possible to minimize being targeted. Two Jagdpanthers were to be stationed forward at all times, with the remainder of the platoon close enough to participate in an engagement, and combine firepower. On encountering AT fire, movement and rapid engagement were key, and individual Jagdpanthers were to avoid engaging until additional armour arrived.

During an attack, the Jagdpanther was to support initial encounters by engaging the heaviest enemy armour, tying them down to make them vulnerable to additional attacks from the front and rear, and protect one or both friendly flanks during such engagements. When supporting infantry, the vehicles were to operate immediately behind the foremost groups. Jagdpanthers could co-operate with other mobile units during pursuit operations, provided fuel and ammunition re-supply had been secured. In defence, they were to be

The Soviet 'ОТЛИЧНЫЙ ТАНКИСТ' ['Otlichnuy Tankist', or 'Great Tankman'] award was established by a Decree of the Presidium of the Supreme Soviet of the USSR on 21 May 1942, and bestowed up to junior officers for outstanding service related to armour. The 46mm×36.6mm award was partially bordered by oak leaves. Similar badges were presented to other services, including scouts, submariners, and snipers. (Public domain)

kept in close formation behind lines threatened by enemy tank attacks, where ready areas and firing positions had been established, and made the best use of terrain. Digging them into the main battle line was forbidden. When breaking off from an engagement, Jagdpanthers were to act as a mobile rearguard, although their lack of a turret proved a handicap, and recovery was difficult should they become immobilized. When fighting for forests or towns the Jagdpanther was to provide covering fire for the attacking units until they achieved a breakthrough. At night, after in-depth reconnaissance, Jagdpanthers could be used in close conjunction with other weapons in localized attacks.

Jagdpanther allocation to Heer Panzerjäger-Abteilungen

Unit	With platoons	With staff	Replacements	Total
3./sPz.Jg Abt 519	14	3	10	27
1./sPz.Jg Abt 559	14	3	39	56†
1./sPz.Jg Abt 560*	14	0	11	25††
1./sPz.Jg Abt 563	14	0	0	14
3./sPz.Jg Abt 616	14	0	0	14
1.–4./sPz.Jg Abt 654	56	3	49	108
2./sPz.Jg Abt 655	14	0	10	24

* Participated in Operation Frühlingserwachen.
† One Jagdpanther given to 1./sPz.Jg Abt 560.
†† One Jagdpanther received from 1./sPz.Jg Abt 559.
Smaller numbers of Jagdpanthers were allocated into Heer (105), Ersatzheer (2) and Waffen-SS (37) formations – the latter including 2. SS-Panzer-Division Das Reich and 9. SS-Panzer-Division Hohenstaufen, both of which would fight in Hungary – and to the Heereswaffenamt (5).

SOVIET

Having seen the error of rigid, set-piece operations that stymied individual initiative and reaction to a rapidly changing battlefield, by 1944, the Soviets had incorporated Lend-Lease motorized transport and supplies to enable their forces to penetrate deep into enemy rear areas, much as had been inflicted upon them by the Germans three years earlier. As the Red Army's logistics were closely tied to rail lines, a combination of motorized and horse-drawn transport was used to move food, fuel and ammunition from the railhead to the front. Advances were further aided as their ground forces commonly travelled with limited equipment and supplies.

The Soviets primarily used the SU-100 as self-propelled artillery, and not as an assault gun, as was German practice with the Sturmgeschütz. The Soviet guns were intended to be used in the same manner as any other direct-fire artillery, in that they moved into positions to engage targets as would their towed equivalents. They were to avoid close-in assaults, as the T-34/85 and IS-2 were better suited to such roles. Instead, SU-100s were usually held back to support an assault from overwatch positions on the flank or suitable high ground, and as such they were not fitted with machine guns for self-defence. In this role they provided direct-fire support where needed to facilitate a breakthrough. The SU-100's large-calibre main gun could also be used to destroy enemy anti-tank guns, generally beyond effective return-fire ranges.

SU-100 crews focused on achieving surprise and executing decisions quickly. Once fields of fire were established, terrain was to be exploited for protection and concealment. Enemy armour and anti-tank guns were priority targets, and against overwhelming numbers the tankers were to scatter and regroup at a more advantageous position. If hostile armour was sighted, the SU-100 was to halt and prepare to engage them by surprise, holding fire as long as possible and co-operating with other vehicles to apply maximum firepower, especially against heavier AFVs, such as the Tiger II.

SU-100-equipped medium SPG brigades (and regiments)

207th Guards Medium SPG Brigade: 912th, 1004th and 1011th Guards medium SPG regiments*

208th Guards Medium SPG Brigade: 1016th, 1068th and 1922nd Guards medium SPG regiments*

209th Medium SPG Brigade: 1951st, 1952nd and 1953rd medium SPG regiments*

231st Medium SPG Brigade: 1022nd, 1038th and 1051st medium SPG regiments

Other SU-100-equipped SPG regiments

382nd Guards*, 416th Guards, 356th Guards, 381st Guards, 382nd Guards, 389th Guards, 390th Guards, 400th Guards, 424th Guards, 1001st, 1415th, 1453rd*, 1727th, 1818th, 1821st*, 1825th, 1821st, 1049th, 1821st

* Involved in Operation Frühlingswachen.

An SS-Obersturmführer (first lieutenant) wearing an Iron Cross 2nd Class ribbon observing through one of his Panther Ausf A/G's seven cupola periscopes. He and his radio operator each wore a Kehlkopfmikrofon (larynx microphone) Modell B, which minimized peripheral noises, while the driver and gunner each had a simpler Modell A. The entire crew wore Doppelfernhörer (double telephone receiver) Modell B headsets. The Fu 15 and Fu 16 radio sets fitted in the Jagdpanther were those commonly used by the artillery, and not tank units – the Panther, for example, used the Fu 5. Three battalion headquarters Jagdpanthers were each outfitted with an additional long-range Fu 8 set. (NARA)

ON THE BATTLEFIELD

GERMAN

With respect to operating the Jagdpanther, as with other German armour, several guidelines had been developed to allow troops to move and fight in the most effective fashion, although these were to be interpreted using the commander's discretion and depending on the situation. Commanders were to become thoroughly familiarized with the surrounding terrain, and time was taken to pass this information to their subordinates, and attached support personnel. Visually scanning for enemies in all directions was paramount, as was maintaining strict radio discipline, especially between command vehicles – unless in an emergency. While aggression in combat was stressed, unnecessarily risky action was discouraged.

The steering system on the Panther/Jagdpanther was a 'single radius' system that encompassed transmission-mounted 'support' brakes where the drive shafts exited either side of the vehicle, and a second larger variety enclosed in sheet-metal shields near the hull walls. Unlike using epicyclic gearing, clutches and the support brakes to reduce track speed on one side of the vehicle in order to turn in that direction, single radius relied on the turning radius initially being dictated by the transmission gear chosen by

Lieutenant M. Alferov's SU-100 is pictured here serving with 2nd Byelorussian Front near Danzig in April 1945, by which time the Soviets had overrun the city. Note that its radio aerial mount has been wired into an overhead telephone line. For internal communication, SU-100 crews used a TPU-4 telephone/intercom system incorporating headphones within a crash helmet, and a rudimentary throat microphone. Unlike most Red Army tanks (Lend-Lease excluded) that only had a radio receiver, the SU-100 also possessed a transmitter for two-way communication, which promoted operational flexibility among the SU batteries, and with their superiors. The 10-RK radio operated between 3.75 and 6MHz, and comprised a 10-RT-26 10-watt transmitter and 10-RK-26 receiver, with stationary and moving ranges of 24km and 16km, respectively. (From the fonds of the RGAKFD, Krasnogorsk via www.stavka.org.uk)

the driver at the time he began to apply the brake, not the amount of pull on the steering lever. He was expected to judge the sharpness of a curve and shift into the appropriate gear in advance, the lower gears providing a tighter radius of turn. This type of steering required little strength from the driver but a good deal of skill, which was made easier by the hydraulic boost for both the support and drive braking. Sharp, skidding turns could still be accomplished by hauling back harder on one of the brake levers to stop completely that side's tracks via the large disc-brakes. To the far left was another lever hanging down near the sponson wall – this was the parking brake, which effectively locked both disc-brake units once the vehicle stopped. Although the single radius steering was an improvement over the simple clutch-and-brake system in earlier German tanks, the Jagdpanther's weight and commensurate brake torque frequently overstressed its small, double-reduction gear mounts. As this could cause the vehicles to break down during operations, instructions to new drivers stressed that major changes in speed (torque) were to be expressly avoided.

SOVIET

The process of operating the SU-100 was much the same as for the T-34. Drivers could enter their forward compartment head or feet first through the glacis hatch, or (generally for larger drivers) through the turret. Like the rest of the vehicle, the driver's position was very utilitarian, utilizing a plywood seat with no upholstery or ability to adjust to different body types. Because of the darkened vehicle interior, the driver would have his compartment light on. The forward instrument panel comprised temperature readings for oil entering and exiting, and the water leaving the engine. To help protect against the numerous hard interior components, each crewman wore a padded 'sausage hat'.

The starting process began by pressing the grounding button to establish a connection to the batteries. If a cold start, the electric oil pump would be activated, and after a few moments to allow for proper lubrication, the driver would depress the clutch, and then slowly do the same with the accelerator. After pressing the starter button, the noisy engine sputtered to life, and soon settled into a proper rhythm. If no unusual smells, sounds or gauge readings were evident, the driver adjusted the idle via the manual gas lever at his seat's left, and waited until the engine warmed up.

Lacking visibility to the sides, the SU-100 would be driven with the glacis hatch open as much as possible, because with it closed, seeing forward was considerably more difficult. To prevent slipping, the gearshift's locking mechanism needed to be pulled back to the handle for operation, which for cross-country travel was not to exceed first or second gear. Either the left or the right steering handle would be manually pulled back to turn the vehicle in the desired direction. Unlike the foot brake, which applied to both tracks equally, each steering handle disengaged that side's track's clutch, and removed its power, while a hard pull applied a brake that resulted in a tighter turn in that direction. If stationary, the vehicle could rotate nearly in place.

COMBAT

THE GERMAN PLAN

Hitler looked to capitalize on the elimination of the Gran bridgehead by undertaking what he envisaged as a fatal strike against Soviet forces in Hungary, and potentially the Balkans. Wöhler, having recently replaced Friessner as Heeresgruppe Süd's commander, preferred to strike Malinovsky's northern flank from Slovakia as the Soviet commander reorganized following Budapest's fall, but the Führer's unyielding vision for the coming fight held sway. On 22 February, Wöhler presented Hitler with four potential plans on how best to conduct it. Considering the strong enemy presence around Budapest, Dietrich stressed that any such offensive would first need to address this threat to his flank prior to any push south to help trap the Soviet Twenty-Sixth, Fifty-Seventh and First Bulgarian armies between his 6. Panzerarmee and Generaloberst Alexander Löhr's Heeresgruppe E, which was conducting anti-partisan operations as its remnants withdrew from Yugoslavia. With German strength and endurance likely to prove insufficient to conduct a two-part operation requiring a major redirection of effort and a subsequent push 200km into the enemy rear, both his plan and a similar one forwarded by Heeresgruppe Süd's chief of staff, Generalleutnant Helmuth von Grolman, were discarded.

Instead, both Wöhler and Balck presented separate – but similar – solutions in which the pincer operation to destroy Soviet forces west of Budapest be made a secondary concern, in a reversal of priorities. Even though the threat to 6. Panzerarmee's left rear flank would be considerable if unprotected – as, should it collapse, Dietrich's command would be vulnerable to encirclement – on 25 February, Wöhler and Guderian

Throughout World War II, the Germans made widespread use of anti-aircraft artillery against ground targets. Here, a whitewashed German 8.8cm Flak 18 with a gun shield is being used in an AT capacity. The two sections of its wheeled Sonderanhänger 201 trailer could be attached to the weapon's framework for transport via a hitched prime mover, such as an SdKfz 8. Its phone lines are in the foreground, and several ready rounds are stacked on the ground. A stopped Soviet T-34 is just visible at the far left. (NARA)

A battery of unguided German Nebelwerfer rockets is launched against enemy positions. Similar to the Soviet Katyusha and able to saturate an area with HE rounds, the Nebelwerfer's frightful noise in flight provided a powerful psychological aspect as well. (NARA)

met at OKH headquarters at Zossen near Berlin to discuss the matter, and agreed to Balck's plan. In co-ordination with *Eisbrecher* and *Waldteufel*, Operation *Frühlingserwachen* was to be the main attack; its primary formation, 6. Panzerarmee, was to strike south from between Lakes Balaton and Velence using I. and II. SS-Panzerkorps, with I. Kavalleriekorps on the right flank. Balck's 6. Armee (IV. SS-Panzerkorps and III. Panzerkorps) would anchor the left, where it was to push east for the Danube. Once Soviet forces to Dietrich's south were eliminated, the full Axis weight would be thrown into recovering Budapest, crippling 2nd and 3rd Ukrainian fronts' offensive capabilities and potentially facilitating the Axis recovery of Romania's oil facilities. To ensure secrecy during the build-up, no details were to be made available below corps level – a determination that greatly confused lower-echelon commands as to their battlefield goals, and how best to prepare for them. While on paper such an endeavour may have held short-term promise, late-war realities could not back it up. Against an experienced, well-supplied enemy, the Germans lacked equipment, trained manpower and armour, and the logistical systems to support these resources.

With SS-Obergruppenführer Hermann Preiss's I. SS-Panzerkorps tasked as Dietrich's right-hand spearhead, *Leibstandarte* fielded 27 PzKpfw IV and 41 Panther tanks, and eight 2cm-quad Flakpanzer IV Wirbelwinde (Whirlwinds), as well as the attached sSS-Pz Abt 501, fielding 36 Tiger II tanks. Each Tiger II had sufficient frontal armour to resist all contemporary enemy anti-tank projectiles, save perhaps the US 90mm HVAP round at close range, and the same high-velocity 8.8cm main gun as on the Jagdpanther; the 70,000kg behemoth had good manoeuvrability for its size, although it suffered from high fuel consumption and gasket-related leaks that hampered operational reliability. While a valuable asset, its bulk made it ill-suited for offensive operations over soft terrain, as illustrated in the Ardennes, and once it broke down or expended its fuel, it was nearly impossible to recover.

Since 12 February, *Leibstandarte* had resided around its Nové Zámky staging area in Slovakia, where it organized its Panzer and Panzergrenadier assets into

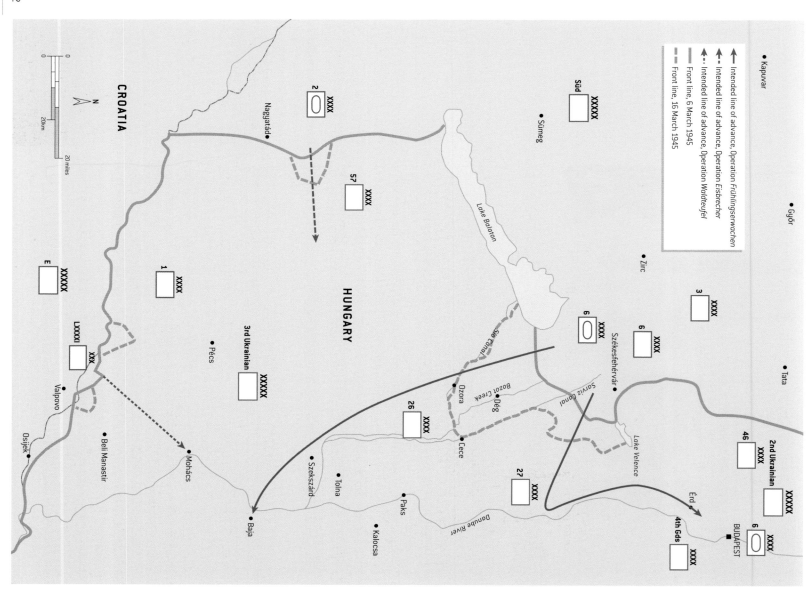

CROATIA

HUNGARY

Kapuvar

Győr

Tata

Sümeg

Zirc

Nagyatád

Lake Balaton

Pécs

Beli Manastir

Valpovo

Osijek

Mohács

Baja

Kalocsa

Paks

Tolna

Szekszárd

Cece

Ozora

Dég

Bozot Creek

Sió Canal

Sárvíz Canal

Lake Velence

Székesfehérvár

Érd

BUDAPEST

Danube River

2
XXXX

57
XXXX

Süd
XXXXX

E
XXXXX

1
XXXX

LXXXXI
XXXX
XX

3rd Ukrainian
XXXXX

26
XXXX

27
XXXX

4th Gds
XXXX

6
XXXX

6
XXXX

3
XXXX

46
XXXX

2nd Ukrainian
XXXXX

6
XXXX

N

0 _____ 20km
0 _____ 20 miles

Front line, 16 March 1945

Front line, 6 March 1945

Intended line of advance, Operation Waldteufel

Intended line of advance, Operation Eisbrecher

Intended line of advance, Operation Frühlingserwachen

two battlegroups, respectively under SS-Obersturmbannführer Joachim Peiper and SS-Obersturmbannführer Max Hansen, both of whom had served with distinction in the division since before the war. To supplement its sister division *Hitlerjugend*'s 40 PzKpfw IV, 44 Panthers and 20 new Jagdpanzer IV, in January sPzJg Abt 560 was attached, which brought an additional 31 Jagdpanzer IV and 16 Jagdpanthers.

Tasked with operating along the Sárviz Canal's east bank, II. SS-Panzerkorps, under the command of SS-Obergruppenführer Wilhelm Bittrich, was to perform similar duties using 2. SS-Panzer-Division *Das Reich* and 9. SS-Panzer-Division *Hohenstaufen*. Like I. SS-Panzerkorps, Bittrich's command had heavy artillery, such as towed 21cm howitzers, and Nebelwerfer rocket-launchers to provide heavy fire support during assault operations. Although tanks were in short supply, numbers of the newer-model *Sturmgeschütz* had been added to the Panzer regiments' second battalions to augment their stocks of PzKpfw IV. *Das Reich* boasted 34 Panthers, 19 PzKpfw IV and 28 StuG III, compared to *Hohenstaufen*'s 31 Panthers, 26 PzKpfw IV and 25 StuG III.

German forces available for Operation *Frühlingserwachen*

Units using Jagdpanthers are indicated by *, with the numbers in parentheses indicating the number of vehicles available/being repaired. The 850 aircraft of Generaloberst Otto Dessloch's Luftflotte 4 supported all three operations.

Heeresgruppe Süd [General der Infanterie Otto Wöhler]

6. Armee [General der Panzertruppe Hermann Balck; 45,000 men and 150 AFVs]

IV. SS-Panzerkorps [SS-Obergruppenführer Herbert Gille]: Hungarian 2nd Armoured Division; 3. SS-Panzer-Division *Totenkopf*; 5. SS-Panzer-Division *Wiking*

III. Panzerkorps [General der Panzertruppe Hermann Breith]: 1. Panzer-Division; 3. Panzer-Division; 6. Panzer-Division (in reserve); 356. Infanterie-Division.

6. Panzerarmee [SS-Obergruppenführer Josef 'Sepp' Dietrich; 125,000 men and 320 AFVs]

I. SS-Panzerkorps [SS-Obergruppenführer Hermann Preiss]: 1. SS-Panzer-Division Leibstandarte-SS *Adolf Hitler*; 12. SS-Panzer-Division *Hitlerjugend** [sPzJg Abt 560: 6/0].

II. SS-Panzerkorps [SS-Obergruppenführer Wilhelm Bittrich]: 2. SS-Panzer-Division *Das Reich** [II./SS-Pz Rgt 2: 6/4]; 9. SS-Panzer-Division *Hohenstaufen** [I./SS-Pz Rgt 9: 10/0]; 23. Panzer-Division; 44. Reichsgrenadier-Division.

I. Kavalleriekorps [General der Kavallerie Gustav Harteneck]: 3. Kavallerie-Division; 4. Kavallerie-Division.

Hungarian II Corps [Major-General István Kudriczy]: Hungarian 20th Infantry Division.

German forces available for Operation *Eisbrecher*

2. Panzerarmee [General der Artillerie Maximilian de Angelis; 50,000 men and 70 AFVs]

LXVIII. Armeekorps [General der Gebirgstruppe Rudolf Konrad]: 13. Waffen-Gebirgs-Division der SS *Handschar* [kroatische Nr. 1]; 16. SS-Panzergrenadier-Division *Reichsführer-SS*; 1. Gebirgs-Division; 71. Infanterie-Division.

XXII. Gebirgskorps [General der Gebirgstruppe Hubert Lanz]: 118. Jäger-Division.

German forces available for Operation *Waldteufel*

LXXXXI. Armeekorps zbV [General der Infanterie Werner von Erdmannsdorff]: 104. Jäger-Division; 297. Infanterie-Division; 11. Luftwaffe-Felddivision.

THE SOVIET PLAN

Following Budapest's capture, the Stavka ordered 2nd and 3rd Ukrainian fronts to prepare for a 15 March offensive to take Vienna, some 230km to the north-west. As intelligence, and prisoners recently taken at the Gran bridgehead, indicated a major German offensive was in the offing, on 20 February Tolbukhin ordered defensive positions and anti-tank strongpoints to be established along the enemy's most likely paths of advance, to a depth of between 30km and 50km. These tended to comprise a mixed group of 4–6 tanks and SPGs, 5–6 anti-tank guns and an infantry platoon. As per the Stavka's orders, under no circumstance were units slated for Vienna to be used, although as Twenty-Sixth Army would likely receive the brunt of the coming attack, it received a large influx of anti-tank artillery in the form of 11 additional artillery regiments under Colonel-General of Artillery Mitrofan Nedelin – some 73 per cent of 3rd Ukrainian Front's 5,535 guns, 2,976 of which were anti-tank weapons of various calibres. From Lake Balaton to nearby Lake Velence, Lieutenant-General Nikolai Gagen arrayed his CIV, CXXXV and XXX rifle corps up front, with XVIII Tank Corps held back as a mobile reserve; this entailed forward division frontages averaging just 3.3km, backed by 24.7 guns per kilometre. To its rear, Twenty-Seventh Army covered the remaining distance to the Danube, using I Mechanized Corps plus XXXIII, XXXV and XXXVII rifle corps; XXXV Rifle Corps blocked the most direct route to Budapest.

Much as they had done at Kursk, the Soviets aimed to absorb and erode the German offensive with predominantly defensive positions, while a large mobile reserve awaited the chance to counter-attack against a depleted adversary. Besides, Soviet commanders assumed that spring flood waters would inundate the terrain over which the anticipated German offensive would attack, meaning the deployment of Soviet armour in the sector seemed unnecessary. By early March, three main defensive lines had been developed, which were interconnected by several intermediate and switch positions. The tactical defence zone consisted of two sets of positions to a depth of 10–15km, which averaged 450 anti-tank and 400 anti-personnel mines per kilometre.

Soviet forces

Units using SU-100s are indicated by *, with the numbers in parentheses indicating the number of vehicles available/being repaired.

3rd Ukrainian Front (Marshal Fyodor Tolbukhin; 407,000 men and 407 AFVs)

Fourth Guards Army (Lieutenant-General Nikanor Zakhvatayev): XX, XXI and XXXI
Guards rifle corps; XXIII Tank Corps.

Twenty-Sixth Army (Lieutenant-General Nikolai Gagen): XXX, CIV and CXXXV rifle corps; XVIII Tank Corps.

Twenty-Seventh Army (Lieutenant-General Polkovnik Trofimenko): XXXIII, XXXV and XXXVII Guards rifle corps; I Guards Mechanized Corps* (17/2 with 382nd Guards, 1453rd and 1821st medium SPG regiments; 46/2 with 209th Medium SPG Brigade).

Fifty-Seventh Army (Lieutenant-General Mikhail Sharokhin): VI Guards Rifle Corps; LXIV and CXXXIII rifle corps.

Bulgarian First Army (Lieutenant-General Vladimir Stoychev): III and IV infantry corps.

Front HQ Reserve: V Guards Cavalry Corps.

Seventeenth Air Army (Colonel-General of Aviation Vladimir Sudets): 965 aircraft.

Formerly serving with Sixth Guards Tank Army in Marshal Radion Y. Malinovsky's 2nd Ukrainian Front, 207th Guards Medium SPG Brigade* (21/1) and 208th Guards Medium SPG Brigade* (63/0) were placed under Tolbukhin's command after the German operations commenced.

INTO BATTLE

Having recently been worn down in the Ardennes fighting and elsewhere, then shuttled to various interior locations for a few weeks' training and reorganization, and then transferred to the Hungarian front, German forces were in poor condition in which to undertake even the limited objectives stipulated in Operation *Frühlingserwachen*. As part of existing security measures, as they assembled north of Lake Balaton German units were deposited dozens of kilometres from their jump-off positions, to where they were to progress largely on foot. *Das Reich's* experience was common, in that it had its training period cut to just two weeks before being put on alert on 2 March – far too

1. SS-Panzer-Division *Leibstandarte's* jump-off positions were located around the town of Csősz, along the Sárvíz Canal. This view to the north shows an environment similar to that encountered on *Frühlingserwachen's* first day. (László Pinke)

In preparation for *Frühlingserwachen*, II. SS-Panzerkorps established assembly positions between Lake Balaton and Székesfehérvár, including the village of Nádasdladány. The region's rugged, muddy terrain and numerous waterways hampered a rapid German advance, and made it nearly impossible to use non-tracked vehicles off-road. (Magdi Gulyas)

little time in which to integrate the inexperienced recruits forced upon the division. As the war dragged on, premier Waffen-SS formations had become increasingly diluted via combat attrition; even with a dedicated, aggressive veteran core, and essentially fully staffed, by early 1945 they were a shadow of their former strength.

To confuse Soviet intelligence, Dietrich remained very visible in Berlin until 1 March, before relocating to Hungary. German forces converged on Lake Balaton during the first week of March, the various formations struggling to get to their designated areas on time, for an operation about which those at division headquarters and below could only speculate, in wintery conditions, and over a poor transportation network. On 5 March *Hohenstaufen's* commander lobbied to postpone the attack for 24 hours; constrained by Hitler's rigid timetable, Dietrich remained adamant that the offensive would start the next day, even though his own command post at Balatonfüzfő had only just been established.

At 0100hrs on 6 March the German offensive got under way, starting with Operation *Waldteufel*, an extension of anti-partisan operations in Croatia, in which LXXXXI. Armeekorps was to establish bridgeheads across the River Drau before pushing north for Pécs and east toward the Danube. Three hours later, 2. Panzerarmee began Operation *Eisbrecher* by attacking along Lake Balaton's south-western edge near Nagybajom, where it quickly encountered strong defences and stalled. To the north-east the offensive's final – and most important – element, Operation *Frühlingserwachen*, began with 6. Panzerarmee's artillery initiating a short barrage to soften immediate enemy resistance, while maintaining a degree of secrecy. With a considerable part of their formations still arriving at their jump-off positions, the Germans launched their final offensive in the East amid blustery, snowy conditions, with daytime temperatures near zero degrees Celsius. Low-hanging clouds largely negated aerial support, and flat, muddy terrain proved a considerable hindrance to rapid movement. As Bittrich's command had not yet arrived, I. SS-Panzerkorps left Csősz to fall on Twenty-Sixth Army; although this Soviet formation lacked armoured vehicles, this was sufficiently compensated for by the presence of numerous, relatively static anti-tank and artillery guns that had been organized into mixed-unit strongpoints.

As *Leibstandarte's* Panzergrenadiers spent the morning clearing lanes through minefields, to its right, *Hitlerjugend* sputtered forward against an active, in-depth Soviet defensive network. After pushing through the foremost Soviet defences in about 45 minutes, reconnaissance elements from II./SS-PzGr Rgt 26 reported a further five defensive belts lay before them, a clear indication that they were expected. By the afternoon, however, *Leibstandarte* had established sufficient paths to enable its offensive to resume, but as its armoured vehicles attempted to operate off-road – the better to engage enemy strongpoints – the excessive mud forced the Panzergrenadiers to advance instead, which without adequate armour support produced slow, unimpressive results. *Hitlerjugend* had scraped out similar gains, with I./SS-PzGr Rgt 26 forcing its adversary to pull back quickly, after abandoning much of the heavy weapons. SS-PzGr Rgt 25 struggled similarly; once it captured Peterszallas, the regiment went no further that day, in part as the difficult terrain prevented III./SS-PzGr Rgt 26 from assisting. By day's end, *Leibstandarte* had taken Hill 149, and by evening pushed into Soponya, but overall results were unsatisfactory as little ground was taken. II. SS-Panzerkorps' attack did not even reach its assembly area until later in the day, and it did not go over to the offensive until 1830hrs, just after dark. Other sectors had similar problems, with III. Panzerkorps having made limited gains before Seregélyes, and along the boundary between Fourth Guards and Twenty-Sixth armies, while 6. Panzerarmee struggled just to advance 2km from its starting positions. Heeresgruppe E's advance managed to secure two bridgeheads across the Drau.

As *Das Reich's* camouflaged vehicles needed to be kept several kilometres from the front to ensure secrecy, some of its soldiers had to march up to 20km in full gear to reach their assembly positions. Subsequently behind schedule, personnel of the division moved through Székesfehérvár along the highway to Aba, which – owing to the open terrain beyond – invited the attentions of Soviet ground-attack aircraft, resulting in casualties. To the south-west, SS-PzGr Rgt 25 continued to slog forward amid snowfall and daytime temperatures of only four degrees Celsius, and muddy terrain that only permitted co-ordinated armoured action by small groups. At 0500hrs, SS-PzGr Rgt 26 continued southwards along the Sarviz Canal, with some of its forward units getting to within 4km north-east of Dég, but it would take all day to gain less than 2km. As General der Kavallerie Gustav Harteneck's I. Kavalleriekorps continued to struggle on Dietrich's right flank, *Leibstandarte* captured Káloz from the south and cut the road to Simontornya, before taking Soponya by a three-pronged assault. With *Eisbrecher* and *Waldteufel* effectively contained by the Soviets, German intelligence was indicating that the enemy were redirecting at least three divisions from these sectors to confront 6. Panzerarmee.

THE STRUGGLE FOR DÉG

By evening, *Hitlerjugend* had advanced to within 3km west of Dég, and after re-establishing communication between its two Panzergrenadier regiments by eliminating enemy forces between them, continued the assault southwards. To assist in capturing this important road hub, the divisional commander ordered sPzJg Abt 560 to assist, in which its six Jagdpanthers and eight Panzerjäger IV would integrate with several PzKpfw IV, Wirbelwind anti-aircraft guns, and parts of the division's reconnaissance battalion, SS-Aufklärungsabteilung 12. Just after midnight, the Germans initiated their assault on Dég, using an armoured wedge in which their respective frontal arcs covered as wide an area as possible to minimize exposure. As artillery targeted Soviet blocking positions, concentrated fire from the moving vehicles, including mortars from

A Soviet column passing through a Pomeranian town, including an SU-76M and an American Lend-Lease Ford GPA 'Seep' (Seagoing Jeep) for crossing rivers. Similar in purpose to the German *Sturmgeschütz*, the light SU-76M – equipped with a 76mm ZIS-3Sh gun – provided much-needed, mobile, direct artillery support, although it had a vulnerable, open fighting compartment to reduce weight. (From the fonds of the RGAKFD, Krasnogorsk via www.stavka.org.uk)

accompanying APCs (armoured personnel carriers), enabled them to overrun the obstruction quickly and without losses. Although the Germans stopped firing, they continued towards their objective across open terrain, in part to avoid enemy tank-hunting teams, which would be difficult to counter without infantry support. As the unit advanced under fire, and at least partially 'buttoned up', orientation was only possible by maintaining visual contact with the glowing exhaust of whatever vehicle was in front; radio communication was useless at night as visibility was largely negated.

With I. Kavalleriekorps holding its ground, I. SS-Panzerkorps' recent, albeit limited, success offered the possibility of a major breakthrough. With *Leibstandarte* having opened the road to Cece, along the Sarviz Canal, *Hitlerjugend* spent much of the day clearing the area around Soponya in an effort to facilitate a push for the Sio Canal, and its crossings at Ozora and Simontornya, with 23. Panzer-Division providing support from the rear. Along its left rear, II. SS-Panzerkorps had stalled at Sárosd, after having travelled a mere 6km, and although the area's roads were improving, German optimism was fading.

At 0500hrs on 9 March, SS-Hauptsturmführer Hans Siegel's sPzJg Abt 560 battlegroup stopped some 2km north of Dég. Taking advantage of the morning haze, he quickly organized an attack plan to surprise Soviet forces around the village. While keeping his six Jagdpanthers in the centre to provide overwatch and command and control, he ordered his eight Wirbelwinde to swing wide to the right, then turn in and attack the village. The remaining vehicles were to spread out wide and then converge on Dég at full speed, without stopping or firing en route. Once the defences were eliminated, Siegel's force was to assemble at the local church.

As the attack unfolded as if it were a drill, a hidden SU-100 suddenly knocked out the lead PzKpfw IV. Siegel abandoned his binoculars for the relative safety of his scissor telescope from inside his Jagdpanther; his gunner, having already taken aim at the offender, awaited the order to fire. Before it could be given, the Jagdpanther's glacis was struck, which ripped away the scissor 'scope and sprayed the cabin with rivets and related debris. As Siegel ordered the vehicle to pull back, a second round struck the right drive sprocket, and the Jagdpanther's front shifted to the left as it slipped into a depression. Although not on fire, its present position prohibited effective control of the attacking vehicles, and Siegel had a motorcycle messenger transport him to Dég, riding in the fresh tank tracks so as to not risk detonating a mine.

By acting quickly and decisively, sPzJg Abt 560 and its accompanying armour managed to knock out roughly a dozen SU-100s, and dispersed several others to the south and south-east of Dég. As these vehicles withdrew across a bridge over the Bozot Creek at the village's southern edge, two had become stuck and abandoned. One of the Wirbelwinde had driven into the village toward the road fork from the north-west when an SU-100 rolled past just 50m away. Although a risky proposition, the German anti-aircraft vehicle fired into the enemy's rear, which blew up the SPG. At roughly the same time, parts of SS-PzGr Rgt 25 and SS-PzGr Rgt 26 attacked Dég and secured the surrounding terrain and the village, where they cleared paths through extensive minefields before continuing. During the evening, SS-PzGr Rgt 25 arrived north-west of Mezőszilas, while II./SS-PzGr Rgt 26 moved up on the left. As the front passed to the south, Dég was the location chosen for the sector's main dressing station.

6. Panzerarmee, with support from 600 Luftwaffe sorties in the afternoon, continued to apply pressure, with I. Kavalleriekorps and I. SS-Panzerkorps reaching the approaches of the Sió Canal. *Leibstandarte* concentrated its advance along the Káloz–Simontornya road to the hills just north of the town, where the Germans were stopped by an enemy anti-tank position near Sáregres, 4km north of Simontornya. In a final push, Peiper's battlegroup reached an area near Simontornya, some 25km from its start line. Behind Peiper, 23. Panzer-Division moved to take Sárosd from the rear, while across the Sárvíz Canal, XVIII Tank Corps counter-attacks pushed II. SS-Panzerkorps back from Sárosd.

SdKfz 251 medium APC and SdKfz 7 medium 8-tonne prime mover half-tracks of 1. SS-Panzer-Division *Leibstandarte* alongside a column of StuG III Ausf G SPGs. The incorporation of tracks helped reduce ground pressure, which provided the Germans a degree of off-road capability to move personnel, supplies and towed artillery into a combat environment across the muddy terrain around Lake Balaton. With thousands of such vehicles produced, many were equipped or armed for specialized tasks, including anti-aircraft, infantry support, bridging and casualty evacuation. [NARA]

PREVIOUS PAGES

As part of the final German offensive in World War II, Operation *Frühlingserwachen*, a Jagdpanther of 9. SS-Panzer-Division *Hohenstaufen* advances between Lake Balaton and the River Danube south-west of Budapest, Hungary. Having left their jump-off position near Polgárdi on 6 March 1945, the ten vehicles assigned to the unit operated in the centre of 6. Panzerarmee's assault toward Sárosd. After having advanced just a few kilometres in two days, and with no air activity from either side owing to inclement weather, vehicle '122' emerges into an open area, in which to make best use of its long-range main gun. Although the vehicle's frontal armour is relatively thick, it was not immune to heavier-calibre rounds. Its commander is peering through his cupola periscope as a pair of 208th Guards Medium SPG Brigade SU-100s approach. As accompanying grenadiers scurry for cover, hidden Soviet anti-tank guns fire on their close target from just inside the woods.

In response to I. SS-Panzerkorps' continued advances, the Soviets dipped into their 207th, 208th and 209th Guards medium SPG brigade reserves; that morning, two regiments of Colonel George I. Sakharov's 208th Guards Medium SPG Brigade were pulled from 2nd Ukrainian Front, and thrown into action just west of Puszaszabolcs to cover German advances at Seregélyes, while its third was held in reserve. While defending the area south-east of Székesfehérvár, 14 of 1068th Medium SPG Regiment's full complement of 21 SU-100s were soon knocked out. Although the SU-100 could not stand up to German 7.5cm and 8.8cm anti-tank fire, during the previous two days, 208th Guards Medium SPG Brigade was responsible for damaging or destroying 14 enemy tanks and SPGs and 33 APCs. Although 3rd Ukrainian Front possessed 407 AFVs, nearly one-quarter of which were open-topped SU-76Ms, their use was prohibited owing to their light armour and armament. On 9 March, Tolbukhin unsuccessfully appealed to the Stavka for permission to use part of Ninth Guards Army to reinforce the rear of Twenty-Sixth and Fifty-Seventh armies, and contain 6. Panzerarmee.

SU-100 and ISU-152 batteries provided a degree of mobility to largely static anti-tank defences. In action, the former tended to engage targets from the edge of woods, or to move from the reverse of hills into prepared positions to fire, before withdrawing to repeat the tactic from another location, often at distances of 1,000m–1,500m. While PzKpfw IV tanks and similar-sized armoured vehicles needed to remain vigilant for such threats, larger German tanks such as the Tiger II and Jagdpanther could generally weather enemy rounds across their frontal arcs at these distances.

By 10 March, *Hitlerjugend* had been whittled down to five weak battalions, and replacement personnel were allocated to make up the losses. Already, seven Jagdpanzer IV and six PzKpfw IV had been destroyed, and sPzJg Abt 560 was down to two Jagdpanthers and seven Panzerjäger IV. At 2100hrs, SS-PzJg Rgt 26 captured the heavily fortified defences around Mezőszilas, and then advanced, even during the night, into the area just north of Igar, some 3km from Simontornya. The open right flank impeded SS-PzGr Rgt 25's advance, and *Hitlerjugend* worked to establish contact with its neighbour on the right via scouting parties. As one got under way from Dég, it encountered a Soviet battalion digging in behind the abandoned village of Lajoskomárom. Seven Soviet ground-attack aircraft moved in, and as their friendly ground force frantically shot identification flares, the planes accidentally bombed them, to which a pair of German APCs added their fire.

With the German offensive now only making progress south-east of Lake Balaton, the Soviets were able to move Lieutenant-General Polkovnik Trofimenko's Twenty-Seventh Army to reinforce Gagen's hard-pressed Twenty-Sixth. They also brought up V Guards Cavalry Corps, and reinforced their bridgeheads across the Sio Canal near Ozora, Simontornya and Sáregres, in part to keep the Simontornya–Cece road open. Part of 23. Panzer-Division moved into the latter area that evening to secure 1. SS-Panzerkorps' eastern flank along the Sarviz Canal. In six days of predominantly infantry fighting, 6. Panzerarmee had destroyed 34 tanks and 145 guns, and removed 21,000 mines.

As part of Twenty-Seventh Army, Colonel Alexander Lukyanov's 209th Medium SPG Brigade had spent much of the day countering German attacks. Although his 1951st and 1953rd medium SPG regiments had suffered casualties, one of the SU-100 battery commanders, Lieutenant A. Kochergi, and two of his subordinates,

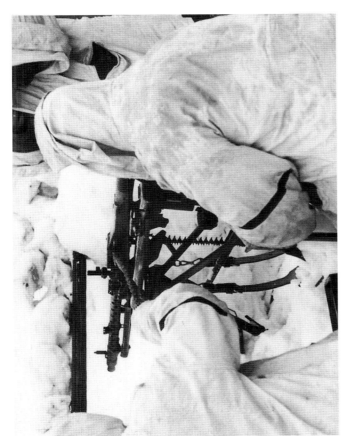

A German machine-gun crew operates an MG 34 in a 'heavy' capacity atop a tripod. The dark armbands were coloured to differentiate between friendly and enemy combatants, who wore similar camouflage. After more than five years of warfare, by March 1945 German formations were no longer able to field and support the necessary amount of combat and transport vehicles to weather attrition, and maintain an effective ratio to support the infantry. As such, during the offensive south of Lake Balaton, their infantry-heavy offensive lacked the necessary mobility and endurance to bring about a victory, however fleeting. [NARA]

2nd Lieutenant Vorozhbitskogo and 2nd Lieutenant Samarin, had destroyed three enemy tanks and assault guns. More impressive, Lukyanov's remaining regiment, the 1952nd under Captain Vasiliev, immobilized three Tiger II without taking a loss. Later that day, 1953rd Medium SPG Regiment was transferred to V Cavalry Corps and given the task of organizing an ambush to eliminate the enemy's effort to break out of the encirclement in Simontornya.

CONTESTING THE SIO CANAL

On 11 March, the condition of lanes and trails continued to improve due to strong winds, even after a very stormy night. While II./SS-PzGr Rgt 26 defended Igar, which was repeatedly attacked by Soviet aircraft, I./SS-PzGr Rgt 26 attacked on the right, and in conjunction with *Leibstandarte* elements pushed to within 2km of Simontornya with the intent of trying to capture the town the next day. The Soviets worked feverishly to secure the Simontornya bridgehead, and launched several small, fruitless attacks to keep the Germans back. 7km to the west, SS-PzGr Rgt 25 struggled to establish a bridgehead across the Sio Canal near Ozora. With sPzJg Abt 560 now fielding four Jagdpanthers, the remainder of Siegel's battlegroup was down to just six PzKpfw IV, nine Panthers and a Jagdpanzer IV.

After an accurate German artillery strike, the attack got going later that morning, with one or two APCs interspersed between the PzKpfw IV. Taking advantage of depressions in the terrain, the group reached a hill some 400m from the canal, where they managed to stay just ahead of Soviet artillery fire. One APC and a number of PzKpfw IV tried to reach the bridge through a ravine dropping down to the canal to

JAGDPANTHER GUNSIGHT

A view through a Jagdpanther's WZF 1/4 gunsight, targeting a Soviet SU-100. The markings indicate the type of ammunition used, and their respective range markings (no machine-gun scale is used). The Jagdpanther used a binocular sight (right: only reticle lines; left: only ammunition range scales), with the two images appearing superimposed when using both eyes. Targeting and firing were to be done only when stationary.

SU-100 GUNSIGHT

Here we see the view through an SU-100's TSh-19 gunsight targeting a defending German Jagdpanther at 800m. In an effort to erode enemy progress, long-range assets such as this could engage armour as well as soft targets, including trucks and infantry. German Panzergrenadiers (not visible here) move behind in the Jagdpanther's wake for safety. Once the SU-100 commander calls out a target type and

location, the loader assembles the proper round and charge and positions it within the breech. The gunner correspondingly uses the telescopic TSh-19 gunsight to estimate range by using the angled mill marks. Once the range is determined the horizontal line is positioned at the correct scale for AP rounds, with the arrow's tip placed over the target.

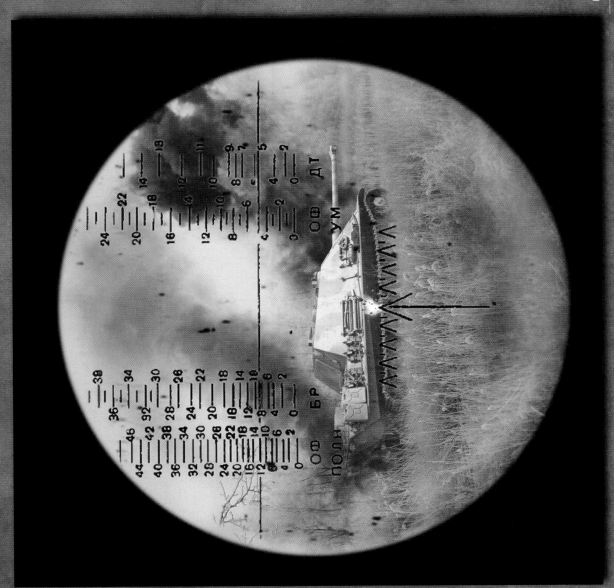

An ISU-152 of 1st Byelorussian Front in 1944, with a sparse covering of camouflaging branches. With a fording depth of 1.3m, the vehicle could remain operational with water up to its return rollers and exhaust openings. Unlike the SU-100, which was designed to engage armoured targets with its high-velocity main gun, the ISU-152 was better suited to attacking bunkers, reinforced positions and soft targets. (From the fonds of the RGAKFD, Krasnogorsk via www.stavka.org.uk)

into the ravine to dismount their *Panzerjäger* complements, while the single operational PzKpfw IV continued to issue suppressing fire and HE rounds, in concert with one of the Panthers. As the APCs evacuated the German personnel, III./SS-PzGr Rgt 26 moved into a rear-slope position, and SS-PzGr Rgt 25 took over the sector.

As part of a final German effort to change their operational fortunes, on 12 March, *Leibstandarte* launched an attack on Simontornya, amid above-freezing temperatures and scattered rain that, again, softened the area's roads. I. SS-Panzerkorps and I. Kavalleriekorps established bridgeheads over the Sio Canal, and surprisingly the latter succeeded in establishing a crossing west of Mezokomárom; despite Soviet counter-attacks the German bridgehead grew to 2km in depth by 3km in width by day's end. At 0430hrs, SS-PzGr Rgt 25 repeatedly attacked near Ozora, but was rebuffed with heavy losses. SS-PzGr Rgt 26 conducted its assault across the waterway to Simontornya's western edge, where the Germans found the railroad bridge blown. Taking the heights to the south by evening, the German advance carved out a bridgehead some 2km deep and 1.5km wide. To the north-east, several Tiger II from sPz Abt 509 achieved success by destroying 20 ISU-152, and assisted a 2km advance, but III. Panzerkorps was forced to assume a defensive stance. Elsewhere, German tanks, including a number of Tiger II, attacked without artillery preparation. During the encounter 1011th Medium SPG Regiment, under Guards Colonel Miller L. Antonovich's 207th Guards Medium SPG Brigade, lost 17 of its 21 SU-100s; this represented the greatest single loss of these vehicles during the Balaton operation. During the fight, however, the formation halted the German attack, in large measure by knocking out 38 enemy AFVs. Considering the number of engagements involving enemy infantry, Trofimenko ordered that from now on his SU-100s were to include machine guns.

Having been ordered to take Hill 220, some 2km south of Simontornya, SS-PzGr Rgt 26 set off at 0625hrs on 13 March; with fire from armour, 2cm triple-barrelled guns mounted on SdKfz 251/21 APCs and artillery pinning enemy forces near their

cover German mine-clearing efforts. As the company commander's PzKpfw IV provided suppressing fire that targeted the inactive enemy positions on the other side once the lead vehicles approached to within 1,500m, roughly a dozen SU-100s from 1953rd Medium SPG Regiment opened fire from the wooded area around Hill 208. With Soviet defenders in strength on the opposite slope, it became clear why they had abandoned recent positions on the north bank. Three PzKpfw IV were quickly knocked out, and a fourth managed to make it onto the bridge before being immobilized. Attempts to tow it from the structure amid artificial smoke failed, as even though the SU-100 fired blind, their volume of fire compensated, making German recovery efforts impossible. Before long, Soviet infantry also opened up, and the two APCs pulled back

With so many waterways encountered during *Frühlingserwachen*, bridges such as this needed to be constructed (often under fire) to support bridgeheads, or to compensate for more permanent structures that had been destroyed. [NARA]

objective, II./SS-PzGr Rgt 26 had reached the hill by noon. The Soviets responded by trying to eject the occupants, but with opposition from *Leibstandarte* elements to the east, they were unable to do so. As 6. Panzerarmee tried to expand on its bridgeheads over the Sio Canal, German intelligence was receiving reports of Soviet activity in 3rd Ukrainian Front, which initially appeared to be a local rearrangement to accumulate reserves. As subsequent reconnaissance flights indicated that a major enemy operation was in the works, Dietrich's command was increasingly at risk of becoming trapped, and the further it advanced, the further it would have to withdraw should the eventuality arise.

Between 0200hrs and 0300hrs on 14 March, the Germans took Simontornya, where they defended both ends of the town's railway embankment. With skies sunny and daytime temperatures rising to 13 degrees Celsius, German armour was finally able to manoeuvre, although by now it was too late to affect the overall situation. Inside Simontornya, *Leibstandarte* managed to reach the southern edge of its cemetery, where a bridge was constructed under fire to cross the 30m-wide, 4m-deep canal. I. Kavalleriekorps tenaciously held its bridgehead against repeated armour attacks, which provided room for the hard-pressed I. SS-Panzerkorps to capture Hill 115, some 2km to the south-east, and expand this bridgehead to include a crossing over the Sarviz Canal near Cece – but only after the bridge was completed, and 23. Panzer-Division had secured Seregélyes. Although the Soviets established a small bridgehead over the Sio Canal near Ozora, SS-PzGr Rgt 25 contained it. The situation would soon change as intensified Soviet counter-attacks prompted Peiper's relocation further north, near Dég, to serve as a mobile reserve. To the north-east, XXIII Tank Corps assisted by SU-100 units pushed the Germans back as far as 3km.

THE DRIVE FOR VIENNA

Starting on 15 March, Heeresgruppe Süd reorganized over the next few days; the Soviets put the time to good use by bringing in fresh units and additional matériel. Although Balck considered the situation in his sector favourably, Dietrich believed the entire operation had failed, and advocated moving to the defensive. Heeresgruppe Süd responded by ordering 6. Panzerarmee to move I. SS-Panzerkorps quickly to its east wing. The bridgeheads at Ada, recently acquired by *Das Reich*, and Simontornya were to be held, while further attacks were only to be hinted at. Already, high-level German discussions were being conducted, arguing the merits either of pulling out I. and II. SS-Panzerkorps on 20 March (similar to Dietrich's original plan), or to halt the offensive. At 2130hrs, Hitler authorized the proposed regrouping.

On 30 March 1945, just prior to the Soviet assault on Vienna, elements of 3rd Ukrainian Front pushed through Schwarzenbach, some 70km south of the Austrian capital, against an ad hoc German defence, including units of I. SS-Panzerkorps. Normally a force modifier, the rugged terrain evident here impeded vehicle recovery, resupply and command and control. (Magdi Gulyas)

OPPOSITE

A tactical view of the outcome of Operation *Frühlingserwachen*, focusing on the sector between Lake Balaton and the River Danube. While German efforts from the south and east produced miniscule gains, their effort between Lakes Balaton and Velence penetrated some 40km, before Soviet forces threatened their deep flank, forcing the Germans to halt, and abandon their gains.

Although 6. Panzerarmee remained a powerful force, by 16 March its continued presence south of Lake Balaton had become untenable. At 1430hrs, the Soviet 2nd and 3rd Ukrainian fronts conducted an intensive artillery barrage ahead of their offensive against Heeresgruppe Süd, and a subsequent advance on Vienna. Forty-Sixth Army followed by striking Hungarian 1st Hussar Division, which was thinly spread along a 20km front in the Vertes Mountains. A Soviet force consisting of Fourth and Ninth Guards armies, with Sixth Guards Tank Army – which alone had 423 armoured vehicles – similarly attacked IV. SS-Panzerkorps and Hungarian 2nd Tank Division between the Vertes and Székesfehérvár, with the intent of pushing north of Lake Balaton and crushing 6. Panzerarmee between it and Twenty-Sixth and Twenty-Seventh armies to the south. While IV. SS-Panzerkorps held its ground, Hungarian 1st Hussar Division did not, but it did not matter at this stage. Although Wöhler believed *Frühlingserwachen* still held promise, between 6 and 13 March, German casualties had amounted to 14,818 (2,451 killed, 11,116 wounded and 1,251 missing/captured), and the Axis troops' will to continue a seemingly hopeless fight dwindled.

At 0120hrs on 17 March, Generaloberst Heinz Guderian, now Chef des Generalstabes des Heeres (Chief of the Army General Staff), telephoned Wöhler's chief of staff, to express his concern about the unfolding Soviet offensive, and to prepare I. SS-Panzerkorps to move to the north-east, and not due east of the Sárviz Canal. A message from the Führer's headquarters at 0240hrs made it clear that the reorientation was not yet needed; such assets would probably be used to stem the enemy tide north of the Danube. Within a few days, the decision proved valid as German units were pulled from their minor penetrations, and sent north to block the route to Vienna, and points west. Angered by the operation's failure, on 23 March Hitler punished the participating Waffen-SS formations by ordering the removal of their distinguishing cuff-titles; most commanders refrained from passing this order along.

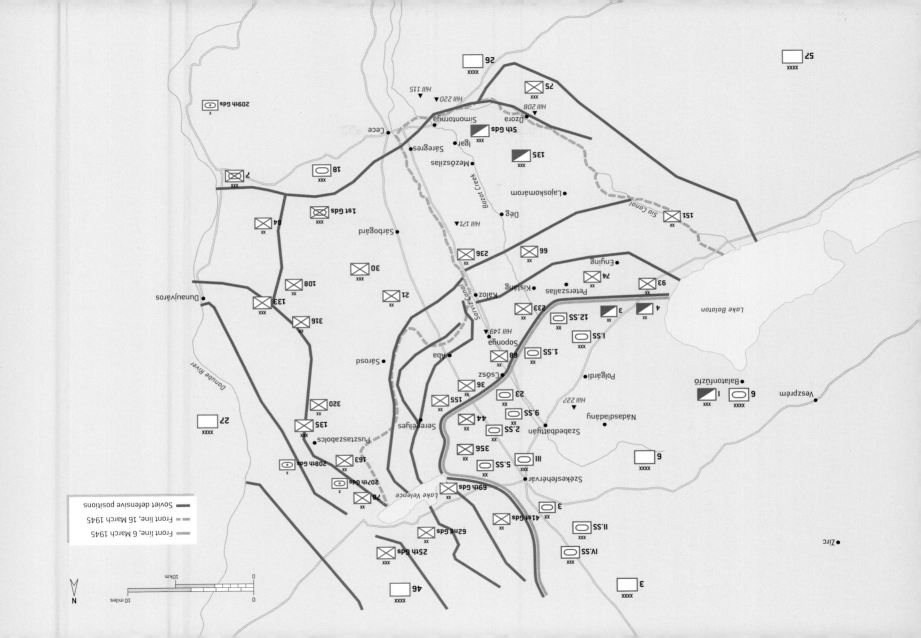

STATISTICS AND ANALYSIS

GERMAN

At the start of World War II, a variety of distinct artillery and vehicle types were fielded to address different battlefield eventualities. For the Germans, the relatively short campaigns between 1939 and 1941 did not unduly affect the strength of their armoured assets, and in fact, the use of captured vehicles meant that when they unleashed Operation *Barbarossa* in mid-1941, their armoured force was the largest it had ever been in numerical terms. In its aftermath, however, combat losses and the distances involved placed an unsustainable attritional and logistical strain on building and supporting a myriad of vehicle types, and related components. With resources soon stretched thinly – a problem compounded by Hitler's decision to create additional armoured divisions by stripping vehicles from existing formations, which offset the carefully conceived unit balance between administrative, supply and fighting components – outdated chassis were repurposed for continued use, and factories moved to streamline their respective processes.

As manufacturing processes matured, and armour and armament increased, the practice of fielding separate SPGs for infantry support and anti-tank duties lapsed; indeed, the Germans often replaced tanks with SPGs due to production shortages or battlefield losses. As part of the seemingly perpetual arms race on the Eastern Front, in which both sides attempted to field a technologically, structurally or numerically superior weapon system – however fleetingly – the Soviets similarly moved to erase the

A knocked-out Jagdpanther from Kampfgruppe 'Paffrath' (1./sPz.Jg Abt 654) alongside a similarly disabled US M36 of the 629th Tank Destroyer Battalion some 5km east of Remagen, Germany on 17 March 1945, four days after the engagement. Instead of mounting anti-tank guns in fixed superstructures, the Americans favoured turreted designs, especially on the ubiquitous M4 chassis. Note the hull penetration just behind the superstructure. (NARA)

distinction between infantry-support and anti-tank vehicle designs. Unlike the doctrine of the United States, in which tanks and tank destroyers continued to operate against discrete target types – at least until the advent of the M26 Pershing – the fact that larger-calibre German and Soviet armour could fire AP and HE rounds made further distinctions unnecessary.

As the Germans transitioned through ever-larger, more powerful anti-tank guns, the cost-effectiveness of simplified designs and increased production made it logical to mount them on the chassis of existing armoured vehicles. Flexibility, a characteristic of all German organizations, was especially apparent in the make-up of anti-tank units, in part as they were employed in support of other arms, and altered their composition according to the task. As German military philosophy stressed offensive operations – in contrast to defensive operations, which were essentially seen as a transitional phase from which to launch new attacks and were mounted by relatively static towed anti-tank guns that could effectively engage three armoured vehicles at most before being overwhelmed – mobility was paramount. With the increasing number of SPGs being fielded, it was realized that guns need no longer lie in wait for armoured attack, but could seek out enemy vehicles. Every soldier was impressed with the ability of new weapons and methods to destroy tanks; something reflected in German service by the name change from *Panzerabwehr* (defence) to *Panzerjäger* (offensive/defence). As such, tank-hunting units were to use their mobility to achieve surprise and provide

Between November 1944 and April 1945, MNH produced 1,838 Panthers and 112 Jagdpanthers. Seen here on 1 May 1945, US Ninth Army personnel examine the bombed-out factory, containing Panther Ausf G turrets (with red-oxide primer or dark-yellow paint), and related components. Note the late-model Jagdpanther (centre) and associated mantlets (bottom right). (NARA)

concentrated fire to actively destroy enemy armour and anti-tank guns. Those friendly towed anti-tank guns that were available would be emplaced in more static camouflaged positions to offer forward flank protection.

Prosecuting a three-front war with logistics spread over hundreds of kilometres severely hampered Germany's ability to fight effectively. What qualitative and quantitative production advantage Germany may have possessed over the Soviet Union between 1939 and 1942 had by 1943 been lost as the Soviets, in large measure possessing industrial assets beyond the range of enemy bombers, could operate unimpeded. Until the Allied bombing campaign began to cause severe damage in late 1944, under Speer's direction the Germans coped by scaling down their production facilities and dispersing them to minimize disruptions – although this meant additional problems as vehicle components had to be shuttled to various areas for assembly. By the time German arms production got onto a proper war footing, it was already too late.

The Jagdpanther's primary deficiency was its lengthy main gun, which unduly stressed the forward suspension. As early vehicles used the unmodified final drive derived from the Panther, they frequently broke down. Although the problem was apparently fixed in October 1944, it continued to plague Jagdpanthers. Reliability proved a concern as well, due to a vehicle life expectancy of just 500km. As with other German armoured vehicles, the Jagdpanther relied on a petrol engine, which was more complex to build than similar diesel designs, and resulted in higher maintenance and production costs. Although the Germans intended to rectify the problem in 1941, the time and effort required to convert the German economy over to diesel engines was prohibitive. Although saddled with a few minor design issues, the Jagdpanther was only as good as its support system would permit. As the war drew to a close, Jagdpanthers were commonly assigned tasks for which they were not designed, including use as infantry-supporting assault guns, individual tactical deployments, or positioned to the rear of a fighting withdrawal, in which if the Jagdpanther was immobilized it would commonly be left behind. In the case of sPzJg Abt 560, being attached to *Hitlerjugend*'s SS-Pz Rgt 12 meant recovery was undertaken at that level, with vehicles organic to the Panzer regiment receiving preferential treatment.

Although only 419 Jagdpanthers were produced during the war's final 15 months, its balance of armour protection, firepower and manoeuvrability made it a very successful design against contemporary enemy armour, especially when undertaking engagements at long range. As an indication of the Jagdpanther's and Panther's battlefield success, both types served in the French Army into the 1950s.

Ammunition penetration statistics

These tables present the penetration (in millimetres) achieved by the projectiles used by the two types' main guns of rolled homogeneous armour at 0° and 30° (separated by a forward slash in each case) at ranges from 100m to 2,000m. Although these figures are derived from period Allied and German testing documentation, they cannot be considered completely accurate due to deviations in plate manufacturing and composition, penetration criteria and ammunition quality. The Germans considered a projectile as having penetrated if at least 50 per cent had passed behind the plate, while Soviet calculations took 75 per cent as the benchmark.

8.8cm PaK 43/3 L/71 (Jagdpanther)

	100m	500m	1,000m	1,500m	2,000m
Pzgr 39/43 (APCBC-HE)	233/202	219/185	204/165	190/148	176/132
10.4kg (warhead); 23.35kg (total); 1,018 m/sec					
Pzgr 40/43 (HVAP/-T)	274/237	251/217	223/193	211/170	184/152
7.3kg (warhead; total weight not known); 1,130m/sec					
Gr 39/43 HI (HEAT)	90/90	90/90	n/a	n/a	n/a
7.65kg (warhead); 16kg (total); 600m/sec					

100mm D-10S L/56 (SU-100)

	100m	500m	1,000m	1,500m	2,000m
BR-412 (APHE-T)	n/a	155/125	135/110	115/95	100/80
15.88kg (warhead), 30.1kg (total); 895, 897 or 880m/sec					
BR-412B (APHE-T)	n/a	160/130	150/120	135/110	125/100
15.88kg (warhead), 30.1kg (total); 897m/sec					

SOVIET

An economic base must be sufficiently developed to survive a prolonged conflict. The USSR had built up a much more effective and reliable economic infrastructure since the 1920s when compared to the German economy. Because of all of the economic help the United States (and Germany to a lesser extent) provided to the USSR during the 1930s, Soviet industrial capacity had advanced considerably in just a decade, and was well suited to the production of large numbers of simple, generally rugged military vehicles.

As an up-gunned iteration of the Soviet SU-85 (and the T-34), the SU-100 possessed the structural qualities that made the tank version successful, including sloped armour, reliability and firepower. To produce and maintain the SU-100 in the field, and enable

A Soviet SU-100 commemorative stamp, as part of a five-piece set that included the ISU-152, KV-1, IS-2 and T-34/76. It reads 10K (kopecs) / Mail USSR/ 1984 along the side, and SU-100 Medium Self-Propelled, Victory Weapon, and Patriotic War, in the upper right. Designed by G. Komlev, only 3,600 were released, on 25 January 1984. (Public domain)

An SU-100 participating in the 2010 Victory Day parade rehearsal in Moscow. The wreath, red star and flag (with 'гвардия') indicates a vehicle from a Guards unit, with a '222' tactical identification number. A pair of more modern Buk-M1 Air Defense System vehicles are in the background: Transporter Erector Launcher 9A310M1 (left)/ 9A39M1 Loader-Launcher (centre). (Vitaly Kuzmin)

the Red Army in general to conduct an effective war. Allied Lend-Lease was of primary importance. In addition to supplying foodstuffs sufficient to feed ten million people for 1,688 days, 92 per cent of all railroad locomotives, rolling stock and rails, 74 per cent of all truck transport, 88 per cent of all radio equipment and over 60 per cent of all automotive fuel, it provided over half the USSR's high-grade steel.

The SU-100 achieved optimal results when used in five-vehicle batteries from overwatching ambush positions, a tactic that had been used with the SU-85 to good effect. Typically, an engagement was conducted from just inside a forest or on a reverse slope, at essentially point-blank ranges of 100–200m. An officer, usually in an SU-76 or T-34/85, provided observation and control. Usually, the SU-100 engaged targets at

1,000–1,300m, which proved sufficient to cripple a PzKpfw IV, and badly damage a Panther or Tiger II, and possibly crack, or otherwise damage their armour's integrity. The 100mm main gun was a marked improvement over the 85mm, although its rate of fire was reduced from 5–6 per minute to 3–4, a deficiency partially compensated for by its greater shot mass. The SU-100's frontal armour proved virtually invulnerable to light and medium rounds, but was susceptible to fracturing when struck by an 8.8cm anti-tank projectile at normal ranges.

Like the Jagdpanther, the SU-100 was very front-heavy, which resulted in excessive stress on the forward road wheels that risked mechanical failure. Never a Red Army priority, crew comfort was an afterthought, and the vehicle's cramped interior hampered effectiveness. Many in the field felt that the SU-100 would do better if partnered with a 152mm gun, as on the ISU-152, to which a report countered that the 100mm SPGs were the most effective means to deal with contemporary heavy enemy armour. The vehicle could run on either petrol or less flammable diesel, which enhanced operational flexibility. Between September 1944 and the end of April 1945, 1,350 were produced – more than three times the number of Jagdpanthers. After World War II and into the 1970s, the SU-100 continued to see service with the armed forces of several Warsaw Pact and Soviet-supported countries, including Egypt, China and Vietnam.

AFTERMATH

Following the Axis withdrawal into Austria, and the siege of Vienna (2–14 April 1945), German forces were hard pressed to organize effective resistance, with domestic production of fuel, ammunition, spare parts and other necessities of war severely degraded due to aerial bombing, or declining logistics capabilities as ever greater

An ISU-122 in Vienna, April 1945. With ISU hull production outpacing that of 152.4mm ML-20S howitzers, the Soviets decided to incorporate the 122mm A-19S cannon as a more dedicated AT option. Operationally, it was used to engage both fixed and armoured targets, but its two-piece ammunition reduced its effectiveness, and made it unsuitable for fast-moving actions. A variant of its 122mm gun was used in the IS-2 heavy tank. (From the fonds of the RGAKFD, Krasnogorsk via www. stavka.org.uk)

SU-100s and T-34/85s in the Berlin sector on 30 April 1945. The white horizontal stripes are for aerial friend-or-foe identification. While the diamond-shaped tactical symbol was commonly used until the war's end, the corresponding unit and vehicle numbering system had little consistency, in large measure to confuse German intelligence. (Public domain)

numbers of supply-service personnel were pressed into combat duties. Vehicles that broke down were destroyed or abandoned on the spot by their crews. With the war lost, German commanders, especially in the East, tended to continue fighting, in part to hold on long enough to surrender to the less vengeful Western Allies, but also to enable as many civilians as possible to escape the Soviet onslaught.

Having remained at the Oder and Neisse rivers for three months, on 16 April the Red Army initiated an advance on Berlin via the Seelow Heights. Within five days, the Soviets had fought their way into the outskirts of the German capital, while 1st and 2nd Byelorussian and 1st Ukrainian fronts conducted a pincer movement to encircle the prize. Furious at his subordinates for their inability to stem the enemy tide, on 22 April Hitler refused the opportunity to relocate to a 'National Redoubt' in the Bavarian Alps, and instead, chose to remain in his Berlin, to 'lead' the city's defence until the end. After a failed attempt to redirect forces from the west to help stabilize the Berlin sector, the fighting in central Germany was increasingly ad hoc. Although Hitler had previously ordered Speer to ensure that all German military, industrial and communication assets were destroyed to prevent their use by the enemy, the nihilistic 'Nero Decree' was not carried out, as the Minister of Armaments and War Production hoped to retain these assets for Germany's postwar use.

Having suffered considerable losses at Budapest, Warsaw and elsewhere, the Soviets were aware that their remaining manpower needed to be husbanded for the final campaigns against Berlin and Vienna. Additional forces from overrun nations, and freed prisoners of war helped compensate for this deficiency. Having pushed around Berlin from the north and south, the Red Army encircled it on 24 April, while in northern Italy, Allied forces fought their final engagements near Bologna, which effectively ended that sector's fighting. The next day, Soviet and Allied forces met at the River Elbe in central Germany, some 70km west of Berlin, and the northern half of the Reich was soon overrun. To the south, Malinovsky and Tolbukhin's efforts had kept Dietrich's command (designated 6. SS-Panzerarmee after 2 April) from participating in Berlin's defence, which finally collapsed on 2 May. While the Allies and Soviets mopped up northern Germany, fighting continued in Czechoslovakia and Austria. As formal surrender negotiations commenced at Reims, France on 5 May, the Soviets conducted their brief Prague Offensive, with assistance from Czech partisans. On 7 May Germany officially surrendered, followed four days later by the remaining holdout, Heeresgruppe Mitte in Czechoslovakia.

BIBLIOGRAPHY

PRIMARY SOURCES

BIOS. *German Tank Armour*. Final Report #653. 1946.

Briggs, Charles W. et al. *The Development and Manufacture of the Types of Cast Armor Employed by the US Army during WWII*. US Ordnance Corps, 1942.

Hoffschmidt, E.J. & Tantum IV, W.H., eds. *Tank Data* (Aberdeen Proving Grounds Series). WE Inc., 1969.

Ivory, W. & Rees, W.H.B. *German Steel Armour Piercing Projectiles and Theory of Penetration*. BIOS Final Report #1343, 1945.

NII-48, Sverdlovsk. *Report of the artillery tests of the armour protection of IS-85 and IS-122*. 1944.

People's Commissariat for Defence, USSR. *Combat Regulations for Tank and Mechanized Forces of the Red Army*. Parts I (Platoon and Company) and II (Battalion, Regiment, Brigade). 1944.

People's Commissariat of Heavy Industry, USSR. *Heavy tanks and SP guns in action*. 1945.

Reed, E.L. & Kruegel, S.L. *A Study of the Mechanism of Penetration of Homogeneous Armour Plate*. Watertown Arsenal Laboratory: MA, 1937.

SECONDARY SOURCES

Babadzhanian, Hamazasp. *Tanks and Tank Forces*. Moscow: Voenizdat, 1970.

Beryatinskiy, Mikhail. *Self-propelled Guns: Together with Tanks*. Moscow: Eksmo Iauza, 2007.

Bird, Lorrin R. & Livingston, Robert. *World War II Ballistics: Armor and Gunnery*. Albany, NY: Overmatch Press, 2001.

GenSdH/Rm.f.Rü.u.Kr.Prod. Nr.114/45 g.Kdos.. Berlin: Reichministerium für Rüstung und Kriegsproduktion, 1945.

GenSdH/Rm.f.Rü.u.Kr.Prod. Nr.154/45 g.K. Berlin: Reichministerium für Rüstung und Kriegsproduktion, 1945.

Generalinspekteur der Panzertruppe. *Vorläufige Richtlinien für den Einsatz der schweren Panzerjäger V 'Jagdpanther'*. Berlin: Hauptquartier der OKH, 1944.

Hahn, Fritz. *Waffen und Geheimwaffen des deutschen Heeres 1933–1943 Band 1 & Band 2*. Bonn: Bernard & Graefe Verlag, 1987.

Jentz, Thomas L. & Doyle, Hilary L. *Panzer Tracts No.9 – Jagdpanzer – Jagdpanzer 38 to Jagdtiger*. Darlington, MD: Darlington Productions, Inc., 1997.

Jentz, Thomas L. & Doyle, Hilary L. *Panzer Tracts No.23 – Panzer Production from 1933 to 1945*. Boyds, MD: Panzer Tracts, 2011.

Kurochkin, P.A., ed. *The Combined Arms Army in the Offensive*. Moscow: Voenizdat, 1966.

Leandoer, Andreas. *Jagdpanther: Design, Production, Operations*. Solna: Leandoer & Eckholm, 2008.

Losik, O.A. *The Formation and use of Soviet tank forces in the years of the Great Patriotic War*. Moscow: Voenizdat, 1979.

Maier, Georg. *Drama between Budapest and Vienna: The Final Fighting of the 6th Panzer-Armee in the East – 1945*. Winnipeg: J.J. Fedorowicz Publishing, Inc., 2004.

Markowscy, A. et al. *SdKfz 173 Jagdpanther*. Gdansk: AJ Press, 2005.

Ministry of Defence. *Order of Battle of the Soviet Army*. Part V (January–September 1945). Moscow: Soviet General Staff Archives, 1990.

Munch, Karlheinz. *Combat History of the 654th Schwere Panzerjäger Abteilung*. Winnipeg: J.J. Fedorowicz.

Ogorkiewicz, Richard M. *Design and Development of Fighting Vehicles*. London: Macdonald, 1968.

Parada, George. *Jagdpanther*. Lublin: Books International, 2005.

Pavlov, A.G., Pavlov, Mikhail V. & Zheltov, Igor G. *20th Century Russian Armour*. Vol. 2, 1941–1945. Moscow: Exprint, 2005.

Rikmenspoel, Marc. *Soldiers of the Waffen-SS: Many Nations, One Motto*. Winnipeg: J.J. Fedorowicz, 1999.

Schäufler, Hans & Tieke, Wilhelm. *Das Ende zwischen Weichsel und Elbe 1944/45*. Spezialausgabe. Stuttgart, 2003.

Spielberger, Walter J. *Schwere Jagdpanther: Entwicklung – Fertigung – Einsatz*. Atglen, PA: Motorbuch, 2011.

Svirin, Mikhail. *Stalin's Armored Fist: History of Soviet Tanks, 1943–1955*. Moscow: Eksmo Iauza, 2006.

Svirin, Mikhail. *Stalin's Self-propelled artillery: History of the Soviet SPG, 1919–1945*. Moscow: Eksmo Iauza, 2008.

US War Dept. *Handbook on German Military Forces*. TM-E 30-451, March 1945.

US War Dept. *Handbook on U.S.S.R. Military Forces*. TM-E 30-430, November 1945.

INDEX

References to illustrations are shown in **bold**